A Primer of Psychobiology

SECOND EDITION

A Series of Books in Psychology

Editors Richard C. Atkinson
Gardner Lindzey
Richard F. Thompson

A Primer of Psychobiology

Brain and Behavior

SECOND EDITION

Timothy J. Teyler

Northeastern Ohio Universities
College of Medicine

FREM~1984

W. H. Freeman and Company
New York

Library of Congress Cataloging in Publication Data

Teyler, Timothy J.
  A primer of psychobiology.

  (A Series of books in psychology)
  Includes index.
  1. Neuropsychology.   2. Psychobiology.   I. Title.
II. Series.   [DNLM: 1. Behavior.   2. Psychophysiology.
WL 102 T356p]
QP360.T45   1984   152   83-20642
ISBN 0-7167-1459-0
ISBN 0-7167-1460-4 (pbk.)

Printed in the United States of America

9 8 7 6 5 4 3 2 1

For Erik Teyler, my son

Contents

Preface

This is a book about the brain and behavior. The brain is a most fascinating organ, and I enjoy sharing with others the excitement I feel when considering its intricacies. Indeed, I hope others will enjoy reading this book as much as I enjoyed writing it.

A Primer of Psychobiology grew out of an introductory course in psychobiology that I taught at the University of California, Irvine. The course was designed for and limited to nonbiology majors. Thus, I faced the job of telling dance majors, English majors, and physics majors about the brain and behavior. For this reason, the book presupposes little or no specialized knowledge on the part of the reader.

Because I was writing for nonbiologists and for those in the early stages of psychological or biological education, I tried to keep jargon and specialized terminology to a minimum and to present readable, enjoyable, and informative text with a clear elaboration of concepts.

A decade has elapsed since the publication of the first edition of this book. In this relatively short period of time the neurosciences have experienced an explosion of knowledge and ideas about the brain and how it works. Topics that were then considered far too difficult to study are today yielding to the advances coming from brain research laboratories worldwide. Ten years ago terms such as *endorphin, long-term potentiation* and *neuromodulation* were uncommon. Today they are commonplace among brain researchers.

The neurosciences, along with the fields of molecular biology and immunology are experiencing a period of exciting discovery and advance. As a neuroscientist I hope to involve the reader in this excitement and to share what some of the applications of this knowledge explosion might be.

I wish to acknowledge the work and ideas of the scores of scientists who have contributed to the knowledge contained in this book. For reasons of pedagogy most remain nameless in these pages—yet, without their efforts none of this would be possible. I also thank the authors and publishers who permitted the reproduction of their material.

Timothy J. Teyler
September, 1983

Introduction: Brain Biology and the Future of Humanity

A common theme running through media, advertisements and political announcements is the deterioration of our environment and the need to do something about it. Almost everyone knows the causes of pollution and most of us know the means to a solution. Yet, given this knowledge there has been a certain reluctance to act in a decisive and consistent manner. Some, of course, label those concerned about the environment as alarmists. Most people, however, see the continued degradation of this planet as a very serious threat to the future of life as we know it. Some perspective can be gained by using the analogy of a host-parasite relationship. The parasite depends upon the host for its existence. In a classical host–parasite relationship, the balance between host and parasite is a critical one. If a parasite population increases, perhaps because of the declining health of the host, the drain upon the resources also increases and the host is further weakened until it cannot support the parasite population. The host may be destroyed, thus destroying the parasite, or sufficient numbers of the parasite may abandon the host to allow recovery and perhaps a new resurgence of parasite population.

The common flea and the house cat provide an example of such a relationship. If the flea is prudent, it will keep its numbers low enough that the cat is not overly weakened by flea bites and the consequences thereof. However, given a healthy cat (without a flea collar), the average flea generally does not display great wisdom but rather, increases its numbers until the cat reacts adversely. As the infestation increases, the animal will gradually weaken, thus becoming a less desirable host. At this point the prudent flea will "abandon ship" and set out for better territories. If the flea infestation continues unabated, the poor cat will sink lower and lower and ultimately cease to provide any kind of habitat for the flea. Thus, the dumb flea fixes his own fate through flamboyant fecundity!

People are fleas and the earth is the cat. To supply its biological and social demands, the burgeoning human population is putting a severe strain upon the planet's resources. Nonrenewable resources such as coal and oil are gradually being exhausted and renewable resources such as air and water are progressively being degraded. Much of today's impact on the earth is either the result of releasing into the environment vast quantities of nondegradable synthetic products or of overloading existing biological purification systems. Dump sites loaded with toxic chemicals are a national problem only now getting the attention it demands. To a Martian observer these activities might look like a self-destructive attempt to destroy our own ecological niche. Moreover, even a Martian would puzzle over our half-hearted attempts to repair our environment. A flea may not be able to alter its behavior to protect its host: hopefully humans can.

One reaction is that we need to understand humans better in order to explain and perhaps ultimately control our behavior. The traditional disciplines dealing with the study of people and their societies have not been notably successful in understanding them. Perhaps it is too much even to suggest that the brain sciences can play a role in this historical quest. But by understanding the function of the central nervous system, we in effect understand human beings. Perhaps brain biology is a key to a future renaissance of human understanding. Or, like most things of great promise, a potential for misuse that might lead to an Orwellian nightmare. This is, after all, the era of 1984.

This is a book about the brain; more than that, it is a book about what the brain does. The study of the brain as an organ of the body is generally carried out by neurophysiologists and anatomists. The study of what the brain does, that is, the behavior it produces, is generally done by psychologists and others. This book is a survey of a new field—psychobiology—which is a merging of the brain sciences and the behavioral sciences. The field of psychobiology along with this book represent an attempt to understand the brain and behavior.

The aim of this book is to examine briefly the kinds of behavior that organisms are capable of producing. Some behaviors are very rudimentary and uninteresting. Other behaviors are the result of long years of learning. Still other behaviors come to us without any learning at all.

We will look at (1) the kinds of behaviors that organisms display, (2) the biological bases of behavior and (3) what happens to behavior when something changes the operation of the brain. The brain is considered first as an assemblage of neurons, and then as groups of neurons that share a common job and finally as entire behavioral or motivational systems. The last chapter of the book, *Brain and Behavior,* will examine several recent topics in the neurosciences that have captured the imagination of scientists and laypersons alike. We will briefly examine the nature–nurture question, and find that the question itself is wanting. We will examine the "science-fiction" world of brain stimulation in humans and in animals. And we will look at some recent work with a dramatic surgical approach that has given us much understanding concerning the operation of the <u>*cortex*</u>* of the brain.

---

* Throughout this book various terms appear in italic type and underlined. These terms are defined and listed in the Glossary at the end of the book.

Although readers of this book will not emerge as neuroscientists, it is my hope that they will emerge with a somewhat clearer understanding of basic brain functioning and how their daily behavior is controlled in its every expression by the interactions of brain cells.

1

Life Is
Behavior

Innate Behavior

From the protozoans, which consist of a single cell, to the incredibly complex primates, with trillions of cells, one feature is common to all animal life—behavior. All forms of animal life behave with a bewildering diversity of expression. The behavior of some organisms, such as the amoeba, is rather limited and unexciting, except perhaps to another amoeba. Other animals display complicated and intricate behaviors that often defy description and understanding. Human behaviors are among the most complex and difficult to understand of all.

In attempting to understand an organism, we must understand its behavior and the biological bases of that behavior. The perceptive reader will recognize that this approach to the human study, the ultimate goal, is that of a *reductionist*. A reductionist seeks to explain a phenomenon by reducing it to the parts that make up the whole. The biological bases of behavior can be reduced to muscle movements and glandular secretions, which are generally the result of neural activity, which in turn is the result of chemical activity. Chemical activity can be understood in terms of changing molecular configurations, which can be formulated as precise relationships of particular atoms connected at certain submolecular bond angles and can be expressed by mathematical statements. The logical extension of reductionism is the expression of human behavior in mathematical terms. Admittedly we are quite far from the day when this will be done.

A first question to ask in understanding an organism is "What does it do?" Scientists have devised a scheme for ranking behaviors from the simplest to the most complex. Table 1 lists these behaviors in order of increasing complexity. Taxes and reflexes are both simple behaviors, ones compatible with the absence of awareness. A *taxis* is an unlearned movement toward or away from a stimulus. A moth's flying toward the light is a phototaxis, for example. A *reflex* is an unlearned protective reaction of an organism to a stimulus and is often a movement away from a potentially harmful stimulus. Examples of protective reflexes include coughing, sneezing, eye blinks and

Table 1 Types of behaviors categorized in terms of primarily innate and primarily acquired behaviors. Within each category, behaviors are listed in order of increasing complexity.

Primarily Innate Behavior	Example
Reflex	Jerking hand from hot stove
Taxes	Moth moving toward light
Innate behavior sequences	Fighting behavior of tropical fish

Primarily Acquired Behavior	Example
Habituation and sensitization	Ignoring a ticking clock (habituation). Overreacting to an innocuous stimulus when aroused (sensitization).
Instrumental learning	A cat modifying its behavior to control an external event.
Manipulation of symbolic elements	A human reading or writing a book.

limb withdrawal. Some reflexes are not protective. Salivation in response to the placement of food in the mouth, the
rhythmic movements of the limbs in walking and the knee
jerk are all examples of nonprotective reflexes.

An *innate behavior sequence,* a considerably more
complex behavior than a taxis or a reflex, is a complex
sequence of unlearned behaviors elicited by a specific stimulus. To the casual observer, innate behavioral sequences
may look rather purposeful and well thought-out. Consider the fighting behavior of the stickleback, a commonly
studied fish. If a male stickleback spies another male near
his territory who is displaying a bright red belly—a sure
sign of an intention to intrude—he will attack the aggressive intruder. A human might stand in awe of this little
fish, admiring his tenacity in defending his small part of
the world against an intruder. A romantic observer, however, would be disappointed to learn that the fish will
attack virtually anything possessing a red "belly"—including wooden models scarcely resembling fish—in the same
manner. It seems that the stickleback is responding in a
fixed way (by an aggressive behavior sequence) to a particular stimulus (the red belly) and that both the response and
the stimulus are determined by the genetic inheritance the
fish received at birth. That is, a stickleback reared in total
isolation from all other living things would react in the
same way to either an intruding red-bellied fish or a red-
bellied model, thus eliminating the possibility that the behavior was learned (Figure 1).

A similar story concerns the mating activities of a
species of wasp. Upon meeting a receptive female, the
male proceeds with a courtship dance and the subsequent
copulation. Again, a romantic observer would be dis-
turbed to view the male wasp addressing the motions of
the courtship dance and copulation to a piece of paper on
which are spread the squashed remains of a female. In this
case the effective stimulus, known as the *releaser,* which
elicits the stereotyped response is the odor of the female—
and this odor, in any context, is sufficient to release the
male's mating behavior. Do not get the idea that mother

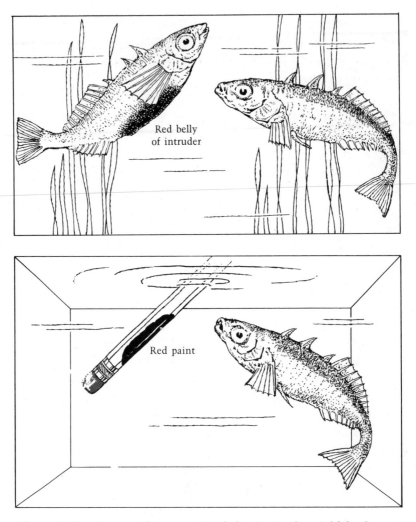

Figure 1 Species-specific aggressive behavior in the stickleback. The male fish will attack an "invading" fish displaying a red belly. Similarly, the fish will attack an object as remote from a fish as a pencil, provided that the pencil has red paint on its "belly."

nature is playing a haphazard game—for a stickleback is rarely confronted with a red-bellied wooden model in nature, just as the male wasp rarely encounters the squashed remains of a female. Because of this, the innate behavior sequences are effective devices influencing the behavior of an organism. Are there innate behavior sequences in humans? The answer to this question is uncertain. Some would claim that the relatively stereotyped human response to a crying baby, the reaction to a scowl from an angry acquaintance or the aggressive response to a territorial invasion may all represent instances of innate behavior sequences.

Reflexes, taxes and innate behavior sequences are primarily unlearned. The behaviors do not develop as a result of practice or teaching—they are inborn. The mechanisms of their actions remain quite mysterious and are only now starting to be revealed (see the article by Kandel and Schwartz listed in Additional Readings at the end of Chapter 1), but it is known that the genetic inheritance that every living thing receives from its parents contains coded information capable of affecting behavior sequences just as surely as it contains a blueprint for the anatomy of the organism. One of the great challenges facing biology is in the unraveling of the "genetic code." Once the mechanism by which information is passed on from generation to generation is fully understood, we will have at our fingertips the potential to eradicate many of the diseases plaguing us today, as there is a sizable genetic component in many of them. We will have the potential for correcting genetic accidents like mental retardation and deformities. We will also have the potential to modify the genetic code and so modify humans themselves.

This is not merely a dream or a nightmare but the form that reality is rapidly assuming. It is only a matter of time until some, if not all, of these possibilities are realities. The potential to change species is an awesome power—one that could benefit us greatly or destroy us. Biologists of the present and future are in the same position that physicists found themselves in during the 1940s, when physicists were working on an awesome source of power—nuclear fission—which could be harnessed for the furtherance or hindrance of life on earth. Some physicists today, as then, feel that the military applications of nuclear energy are wrong and that as scientists they failed in their responsibility to humanity by allowing their discoveries to be used in such a manner. Whether they are right or wrong only history can judge. The point is that biologists are now on the verge of uncovering an even more awesome power. The responsibility for the wise use of this power rests on all of us as it will affect all of society.

Fortunately for life on earth, biologists are well aware of the awesome potential of their work. In 1974 a group of prominent biologists called for a ban on certain experiments dealing with the genetic manipulation of living cells and viruses. This appeal for a worldwide moratorium on research by scientists active in the area was instigated by the discovery of enzymes capable of inserting "foreign" genes into living cells. The scientists were concerned about the possibility that such "new" organisms might escape and infect the population—which would have no resistance to these organisms! The possibility of such an occurrence was the theme of Michael Crichton's science fiction book *The Andromeda Strain*. In more recent years, most scientists have concluded that the potential dangers to which they were reacting were remote. The recombinant DNA experiments, as they are called, have, instead, shown great promise in creating biological molecules of great value to many people.

===== Summary

In this section we have seen that behaviors can be ranked from simple to complex. We have also seen that some behaviors are innate, that is, they are present primarily as a result of genetic inheritance. Most of the innate behaviors humans possess are relatively uninteresting, but important, reflexes. We have seen how some behaviors can be quite precise and elaborate even though they are entirely innate. The expression of innate behaviors is not entirely without environmental influence. Every organism interacts with its environment. This interaction of genetic inheritance and environment determines the final behavioral outcome.

☰ *Learned Behavior*

☰ The behaviors to be discussed below have one point in common: all are learned or acquired, none is inherited per se. A moment's reflection will bring the realization that neither innate nor acquired behaviors could exist in the absence of an organism, and that organisms are built according to a genetic blueprint. It is futile to attempt to separate out a behavior as "purely acquired" because an innate framework is needed for the expression of the acquired behavior. The behaviors discussed below utilize an innate framework, but the specific response to the environment situation is *not* "built into" the organism. The specific kinds of learned behavior discussed below are examples of *behavioral plasticity:* the modification of behavior as a result of experience. Excluded from this definition are behavioral changes associated with maturation, aging and fatigue.

Habituation and Sensitization

Habituation is the reduction of a preexisting response. An example should serve to clarify the meaning of habituation. A sudden noise compels us to direct our attention to the source. If the noise is repeated, we may in time no longer respond to it—we have then been habituated. The opposite of habituation, *sensitization*, produces an augmented response to a stimulus. You may at some time have been sitting in a movie theater engrossed in a suspense film when someone behind you suddenly sneezed, resulting in your jumping out of your seat. That was a sensitized response. Normally the sound of an unexpected sneeze would not elicit such a violent response, but the level of arousal may be so heightened by a frightening movie that virtually any stimulus will elicit a vigorous response. The two processes of habituation and sensitization appear to be basic to all species. A rat giving a startle jump to a loud noise will jump less vigorously if the sound

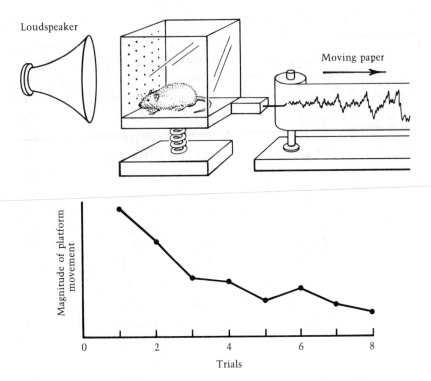

Figure 2 Habituation of startle response in the rat. The rat is suspended on a spring-mounted platform. Periodically a loud tone is transmitted through the loudspeaker and this causes the animal to jump. The jumps are recorded on moving paper, and it is found that their magnitude decreases with repetition of the stimulus. Below is plotted the magnitude of the platform movement versus repeated trials.

is repeated again and again as is shown in Figure 2. Similarly, a male stickleback fish will reduce the frequency and intensity of his attack directed toward a potential competitor if the trespassing fish does not go away. Nerve cells exhibiting the properties of habituation, sensitization or a combination of the two have been discovered in the spinal cord of the cat and the brain of the rat. Habituation and sensitization are particularly clear examples of the interaction between brain and environment in controlling behavior. The innate response is changed as a result of the organism's interaction with the environment.

Classical Conditioning

Classical conditioning (also called associative conditioning) was developed largely by the Russian scientist Ivan P. Pavlov. Pavlov, a physiologist at the beginning of his career, was studying the chemical composition of salivary fluid. To collect saliva for analysis, he first placed a tiny tube into the salivary ducts of dogs. Then meat powder was squirted into the mouths of the dogs whereupon they reflexly salivated. Pavlov's discovery hinged on the accidental observation that after the procedure had been repeated several times, the dogs began to salivate when the assistant who gave them the meat powder on earlier occasions entered the room—before he squirted meat powder into their mouths. The dogs had apparently learned to associate the sight of the assistant with the receipt of meat powder and therefore salivated in anticipation at the sight of him. Thus, conditioning is the establishment of a new response to a stimulus that did not initially elicit a consistent response. Pavlov abandoned his work on the composition of salivary fluids and immediately began to devise experiments to follow up this observation. He and his students studied many aspects of classical conditioned behavior, and such studies continue even to this day.

It is now known that most simple behaviors can be conditioned. The procedure is to associate repeatedly a neutral signal (ringing of a bell, flashing of a light) closely in time with a meaningful stimulus (electric shock, puff of air directed toward the eye, presence of food). The neutral signal will, after a number of pairings, elicit the response that originally only the meaningful stimulus elicited. For example, a rat will normally not respond emotionally to a light. It does, however, respond to an electric shock applied to its feet. It responds in a great many ways: by squealing, jumping, gnawing, urinating, defecating, changing respiration rate and heart rate, and so forth. If a light is turned on just before the application of a shock to the rat, the light alone, after a number of pairings of light and shock, will elicit some of the responses. Such learned responses are called *conditioned responses* and may disappear if the meaningful stimulus is omitted for a period of time (Figure 3).

Such responses as heart rate, changes in skin resistance to electrical current and eye blinks have been conditioned. The Russians have reported conditioning a wide variety of responses, including such improbable ones as blood-sugar level, intestinal contraction and gall bladder movement! On an everyday level, we have emotionally conditioned responses to red traffic lights, hot stoves, police cars, warning signs and the sight of food, to name a few examples. Classical conditioning is thought to bring about an elementary kind of learned behavioral change exceeded in simplicity only by habituation and sensitization.

Instrumental Learning

By way of introduction it should be pointed out that Harvard University's B. F. Skinner deserves the credit for the upsurge of interest in instrumental conditioning in the United States. Most of the behavior that humans engage in daily can be considered as instrumental learning or *manipulation of symbolic elements*. Included in the latter is language, mathematics and the social symbols used in everyday life. In classical conditioning the organism has no control over the course of events. The appearance of the conditioned salivation response, for example, does not prevent or change the delivery of the meat powder. In *instrumental learning,* however, the organism can exert some control over external events. Consider the task of training a dog to roll over. It would be convenient to present a stimulus to which the dog would reflexly respond by rolling over. This stimulus could be associated with the command "roll over." This, you may recognize, is classical conditioning. Unfortunately, there is no such stimulus. Well then, how do people train dogs to roll over? They get the dog to roll over (or something ap-

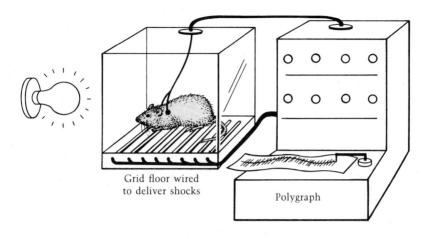

Grid floor wired
to deliver shocks

Polygraph

Early in conditioning

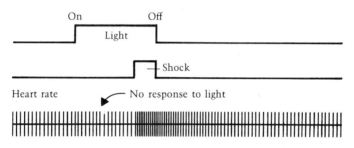

On   Off

Light

Shock

Heart rate   No response to light

Later in training

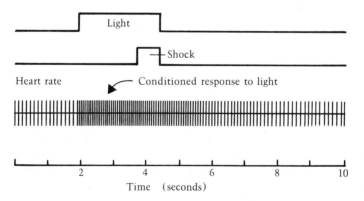

Light

Shock

Heart rate   Conditioned response to light

2   4   6   8   10

Time   (seconds)

Figure 3   Classical conditioning of heart rate in the rat. Electrodes
detect the heart rate of the rat, which is then displayed on a
polygraph. Early in conditioning, the light, which flashes on just
before an electric shock is delivered, fails to elicit any change in the
animal's heart rate. Later in training, the animal's heart rate
increases dramatically each time the light goes on, before the shock
is received.

proaching it) and then praise or give the dog a treat. In other words, instead of producing the desired behavior by a stimulus, they "get the dog to do it" by any of a number of ways, and then reward the action. Since the reward strengthens the desired response, it is called a *reinforcer*. Operationally, we can say that the reinforcer tends to increase the probability of repetition of the response preceding it. Somewhat anthropomorphically, we can say that the animal perceives the reinforcer as desirable and attempts to provoke its reappearance by doing what it had done immediately prior to past reinforcements.

A favorite student laboratory project is to train rats or pigeons to "dance" by using instrumental conditioning. A hungry animal is placed in a testing chamber equipped with a response lever or button and a food dispenser. The "dance" is a rather simple one—going around in a complete circle. The student reinforces the animal (by giving it food) every time it makes a movement in the "correct" direction. Eventually the animal makes a complete circle. Some animals learn the "dance" quite well and will continue to perform until no longer hungry.

The effect of reinforcement can be quite perplexing if the observer is unfamiliar with the preceding events. In one example food was automatically delivered at periodic intervals to some caged pigeons. When observed after a time, some of the birds were behaving in what seemed a strange manner. Some were flapping their wings, others were moving about, some were pecking furiously, some remained in one corner of the cage. It seems that the animals had been reinforced by coincidence for what they happened to be doing at the time of food delivery. Little did the birds know that their behavior had nothing to do with the delivery of food. In this respect the birds were behaving superstitiously. Some people have lucky charms that they believe will help them, while others engage in rituals, both examples of superstitious behavior. We may wonder how many other behaviors are based similarly upon coincidental reinforcements.

Animals can be taught to perform a great variety of tasks by using instrumental reinforcements. A rat can learn to press a bar in order to obtain food. A monkey can be taught to push a button to obtain a brief view of other monkeys at play. Animals can also learn to respond in order to prevent the delivery of an electric shock. Animals can learn to be quite discriminating about a particular stimulus. A pigeon placed in a "Skinner box" equipped with red and blue lights provides an example. Pecks on a button when the red light is on will result in food being made available to the bird. A peck on the same button when the blue light is on will turn off all the lights in the box, an unpleasant state of affairs as far as the bird is concerned. Placed in such a box, a pigeon quickly learns to peck when the red light is on and to refrain from pecking when the blue light is on. The behavior of the bird is under the control of the colored lights (Figure 4).

Human behavior is similarly under the control of external stimuli associated with reinforcers. Most of us refrain from swearing in front of our grandparents and we usually wear formal clothing to weddings. Our behavior is thus controlled somewhat by the external stimuli provided by grandparents and weddings. These stimuli have gained the power of controlling our behavior through previous exposure to the reinforcements associated with them. This is not to say that a reinforcement need occur every time. Gamblers do not stop gambling because they fail to win on each throw of the dice. Motorists do not habitually go through red traffic lights even though they realize that they will not be caught every time. Our behavior is controlled effectively by occasional reinforcements. The same is true of animals in a Skinner box working for a food reward. They can be trained to respond at a high level for infrequent or partial reinforcements. If reinforcements are completely eliminated, both human and animal will continue responding for a long time, presumably because with infrequent reinforcement it is difficult to discriminate when the "rules of the game" have changed.

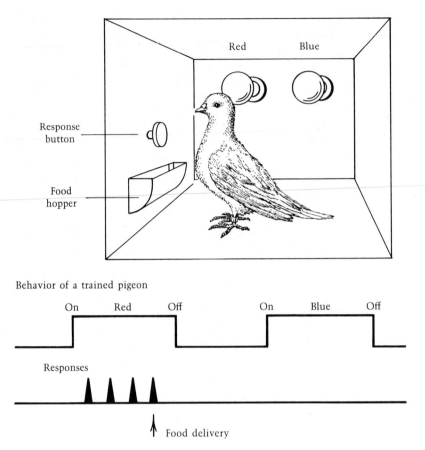

Behavior of a trained pigeon

Figure 4 Instrumental conditioning of the pigeon. The pigeon is in a Skinner box equipped with a red and a blue light. The animal can peck at the response button in order to obtain food. When the red light is on, food delivery follows four pecks at the response button. A peck when the blue light is on turns off all the lights in the chamber—a situation that the pigeon finds aversive. Below is shown the record of pecking behavior of a trained pigeon.

Do these principles of behavior apply to the internal functioning of our body? It is difficult, if not impossible, for most of us to willfully stop or slow our heart. It is equally unlikely that we can alter the blood flow in our left ear. Yet rats can be taught to do these feats with apparent ease. Two scientists, N. Miller and L. DiCara, have succeeded in instrumentally training rats to increase or decrease heart rate and local blood flow. Miller and DiCara have also succeeded in training rats to decrease blood pressure. These techniques are now being applied to humans afflicted with chronically high blood pressure. If successful, the treatment holds the promise of lengthening life and alleviating the misery associated with many kinds of cardiovascular diseases (Figure 5). *Biofeedback*—the "feeding back" or informing a subject of a biological event—is currently being successfully used to provide relief from tension and migraine headaches and to control stomach secretions for relief from the pain of ulcers.

It is often possible to alter a biological response by means of instrumental reinforcements. Biofeedback can be used to modify many physiological events—including internal physiological events of which we are normally un-

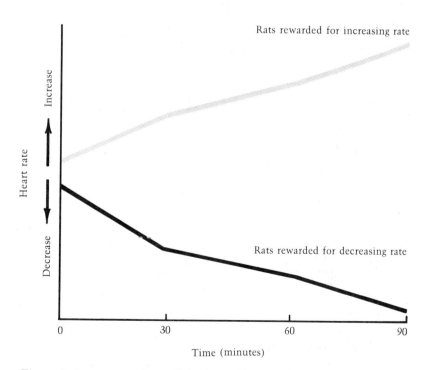

Figure 5 Instrumental conditioning of heart rate in rats. Rats were rewarded with electrical brain stimulation for either increasing or decreasing their heart rate.

aware—and has been most used medically in connection with blood pressure, heart rate and brain activity. Especially with brain activity, there are psychological effects associated with the biological changes.

For many years psychologists had held that such autonomic nervous system responses as heart rate and blood pressure were not susceptible to change by instrumental conditioning procedures. Casual knowledge tends to support such a view. After all, how many of us know persons who can alter their heart rate or blood pressure? The experiments of Miller and DiCara are at odds with casual knowledge in indicating that such training *is* possible. Furthermore, persons from cultures other than our own are capable of altering these bodily functions. Indian mystics and others can actually slow their heart rate and stick pins through their skin without bleeding (an example of local control of blood flow).

In a standard instrumental conditioning situation, an animal may, by responding, bring forth a desirable, or positive, reinforcer or avoid an undesirable, or negative, reinforcer. The organism thus has some control over its environment. We usually structure our daily activities as much as possible to maximize positive reinforcement and minimize negative reinforcement—all by adjusting our behavioral responses to the environment.

Cognitive Behavior

Most of human behavior, of course, does not consist of classically or instrumentally conditioned responses to simple stimuli. Rather, it involves thinking, deciding, reasoning, planning, reflecting and a whole host of much more complicated behaviors. All of these behaviors can be placed under the general heading of *cognitive behavior.*

What do we mean by cognitive behavior? At its most elementary level of analysis, we mean the process by which the brain recognizes and attaches meaning to events in the environment and then utilizes the meaning obtained in some way to control behavior. For example, an object comes into our view. It is red, round, can be easily held in the hand. We "know" these things because, in the past, we had experience with similar objects. We also "know" that this object is called a *ball*. We know not only its name, but we know some of the things that can be done with it: it can be thrown, bounced, a dog will fetch it, it may or may not float in water and so forth.

What I have just described is a very commonplace activity occurring in each of us countless times a day. Yet, the operations that are required to make this behavior possible are exceedingly complicated. The sensory organs must transmit to the brain a neural representation of what the environmental event is like. The brain must then be able to extract meaning out of the sensation. It must be able to integrate the information provided by sensory cues in terms of shape, color, apparent composition and the like, and compare them with information stored in memory as to what this object might be. Once a suitable comparison is made, the organism "knows" what the object is...a ball. The process of "knowing" about a sensation is termed a "perceptual" process. Once this perception has taken place, a whole host of further mental operations can occur. We have stored in our brain a good deal of information about what can be done with a ball, what it is made of, what games it is used in and the like. All of this is accessible to the nervous system once it has made the initial perceptual decoding as to the nature of the stimulus object.

We know that many of the brain operations giving rise to perceptions occur in the cerebral cortex, the thin outer layer of the brain found just beneath the skull. If by some unfortunate accident, portions of the human cortex are damaged, one will often be confronted with a patient who has difficulty in "knowing." Medically, this condition is termed an *agnosia,* which literally means "not knowing." As we shall see later on, various portions of the cortex are specialized for certain types of cognitive operations. In our example, the individual knew that the object was called a ball. Language is a uniquely human attribute.

In most people, the language portions of the brain lie in the left-half brain, or left *hemisphere*. Within the language portions of the cortex, there is further subdivision and specialization. In the posterior language cortex, known as *Wernicke's area,* damage will result in a disturbance of language called Wernicke's *aphasia* (aphasia is literally, "without language"). Damage to Wernicke's area will result in a patient having difficulty in understanding language: written, spoken or sign language. A patient will appear to verbalize fluently, but upon close listening the speech will be disorganized or meaningless. Conversely, damage to the anterior speech cortex, known as *Broca's area,* will leave patients fully able to understand language, but seriously impaired in the ability to produce it; their speech is slow and labored, but the meaning is intact. Thus, we see that the language cortex is divided into regions concerned with the understanding and production of language. As we learn more about the brain, it is expected that this simple division will be revised to incorporate other brain areas concerned with more specific language functions. For example, in both of the aphasias above, patients are able to sing and swear in a relatively normal fashion, suggesting that these functions are not governed exclusively by the language cortex.

Language is only one example of the complex behaviors that humans engage in. Other examples include the ability to form concepts or integrated ideas about things in the environment and the ability to manipulate symbols. An obvious example of symbol manipulation is in mathematics. Other less obvious kinds of symbol manipulation are represented in the ability to play or write music. In fact, it is entirely correct to think of language as the ability to manipulate symbols. The word *ball,* for example, is a symbol that refers to a class of environmental objects and also refers to a set of attributes belonging to those objects.

The ability to represent the external world via symbols and the ability to manipulate those symbols in such a way that communication is possible between individuals is a hallmark of human beings. Learning and using a language, a mathematical technique or a musical score entail not only the acquisition of a vocabulary but the learning of a set of rules concerning the use of the symbols. We know that skills in manipulating symbols (speaking, writing, problem solving, composing) differ widely from person to person, but we do not know why. We know that with training, people can improve their ability to manipulate these symbols, but we are not sure how this learning is achieved. We know something about the brain regions that are involved in the manipulation of symbols but do not appreciate the intricacies of the neuronal operations involved.

We also dream, make decisions, assume responsibilities and perform a whole host of complicated activities—all of which must ultimately come from the brain. For a few of these complex behaviors, we understand something of the brain processes involved.

In years past, it was a common practice to surgically deactivate portions of the frontal lobes of the human brain for patients suffering from severe psychotic reactions. These operations, one of which is a frontal lobotomy, were deemed necessary to control the aggressive and often self-destructive behavior of the patients. It must be remembered that effective antipsychotic medication had not yet been developed. While these operations were successful in reducing aggression in a great number of cases (unhappily not all), there was a noticeable effect on an individual's personality. Goals were no longer as important as they had once been. The controls that operate in most of us and compel us to act in socially acceptable ways were weakened. Some individuals, for example, no longer felt responsible for supporting their families, others had "personality" changes and became strangers to those that knew them. The patients seemed less troubled and concerned about things in the environment that previously had worried them, yet their ability to remember and perform intellectually was not seriously impaired. While it is clearly difficult to precisely define what had happened to these patients, most observers felt that the individual, after the surgery, was very much less a whole human being than before. The operation altered certain very important aspects of what we call personality. Operations removing or deactivating the frontal lobes are now rarely done, as medications are now available to treat these psychotic individuals.

Brain scientists have only begun to understand the neural mechanisms underlying human cognitive behavior. As we shall see in this book, the study of the brain sometimes involves surgical techniques in which electrodes sample the activity of nerve cells or chemicals are injected. The goal is to alter brain functioning while measuring the resulting change in behavior. Obviously, most of these procedures cannot be employed in humans. Since many of the most interesting cognitive behaviors are not present in other species, knowledge will probably come slowly. Nevertheless, it represents a fundamental and fascinating challenge to brain scientists to unravel the brain mechanisms underlying perception, language, learning and memory.

☰ Summary

☰ *Learned behaviors, like innate behaviors, can be classified from simple to complex. One of the simplest of the learned behaviors is habituation, which is not the establishment of a new response, but the reduction of an existing response. The converse of habituation is sensitization, or the increase of a response. Laboratory models of learning include associative conditioning and instrumental learning. Associative conditioning, discovered by Pavlov, depends upon the association of two events in time: the person or animal can do nothing about the events, but simply learns to respond to them. In instrumental learning, on the other hand, the individual's behavior is "instrumental" in bringing about a reinforcement. Instrumental conditioning was given its greatest impetus in the United States by B. F. Skinner. Instrumental conditioning is somewhat more complex than associative conditioning in that the individual's options are much greater, and the freedom to respond in order to obtain a reinforcement or to avoid one is much greater. Human behavior is under the influence of stimuli delivered on partial reinforcement schedules, and these occasional reinforcements are effective in controlling our behavior. Instrumental conditioning techniques have been applied toward changing cardiovascular function in rats and people. The most complex behavior that humans engage in is the manipulation of symbolic elements. By this, we mean language, calculation and abstract thought. Humans alone are capable of achieving great feats in terms of manipulation of symbolic elements. Our knowledge of brain mechanisms involved in this ability is rudimentary.*

The Study of Behavior

The study of behavior can proceed in many different contexts. We unknowingly study behavior every day of our lives when we interact with other people and animals and make judgments about their personalities, intelligence and how we should react with them. Admittedly, this is not a very scientific study of behavior. We are influenced by a good many biases, myths and prejudices that affect our judgments. The scientific study of behavior attempts to eliminate these influences that taint our judgments. This is difficult as scientists are eminently human and carry with them as many biases as do other people. How, then, do they manage to keep these biases from clouding their judgments?

A scientist, when observing a behavior, attempts to describe as precisely as possible the phenomena seen. As measuring instruments are free of human biases, the scientist, whenever possible, will use an appropriate instrument to record and describe behavior. This implies that the instrument is a) accurate and b) that it actually measures what it is purported to. These two characteristics are termed (a) *reliability* and (b) *validity,* and are important yardsticks of the suitability of any measuring instrument, from an IQ test to an electronic instrument. Examples of instruments used in the measurement of behavior range from a simple stopwatch to a large computer. It is important to recognize that while a measuring device may be unbiased, its use by a scientist is according to the scientist's choice. In science, objectivity arises from consensus, and that consensus is provided by the prevailing theories and attitudes in science.

In addition to specifying the response of the organism in precise terms, the scientist must also describe exactly what gave rise to the response. This is also rather difficult because many behaviors of an organism are dependent upon the sum total of experiences that preceded the specific behavior at hand. For example, the avoidance response of a house cat to young children can best be understood by knowing the previous encounters between cat and children. Merely explaining the features of a task that an organism is currently facing is often insufficient because it does not take into account the experiences the organism has had in similar situations in the past—experiences that no doubt affect the behavior of the organism. The solution is to limit the experiences encountered by the organism under test. Our reason for using laboratory animals is thus clear: we can specify the experiences they have had because we have controlled their environment throughout their lives. By choosing highly inbred animals, we can also ensure that there will be little genetic difference among such organisms. Obviously, we cannot be as rigorous for human subjects, or for many animals that have not been reared as laboratory animals. Scientists working with such subjects take advantage of the fact that with a large enough sample of humans or animals, the differences among them due to genetics or experience largely average out. As an illustration, a large sample of randomly selected children will include ones from all racial, economic and social groups and will include some, for example, who were reared with strict discipline and some who were reared leniently; thus the effects of background group and type of rearing on their responses will tend to cancel out when the sample is viewed as a whole.

Many of the factors giving rise to a behavior are set by the scientist at the time of the experiment. For example, the experimenter can place a monkey in a testing chamber in which the monkey can press a lever to view either another monkey or a model of a monkey, measuring the animal's attachment to the two objects. In this case, it is possible to specify quite precisely the physical arrangement and the amount of immediate prior experience with the two objects. A scientist attempts to describe the situation so completely that someone else, when reading of the experiment, could duplicate it exactly.

The last point brings us to a central goal in scientific work—*repeatability*. By repeatability (also called *replication*) we mean the possibility of another scientist's performing the same experiment to verify or invalidate the original findings. The ability of science to describe and explain the natural world rests upon the discovery of universal natural laws that explain some facet of the world. If the repetition of an experiment results in the same findings, then the original observation is given more credence, and if it is never found wanting, it will become part of our "fund of knowledge" regarding the natural world.

There are two basic methods of scientific investigation. One is termed the "field method" and the other is the "laboratory method": both are valid means of discovering the nature of the world. The *field method* entails the observation of a phenomenon in its natural setting—that is, in the field. This method is exemplified in the work of Jane Goodall, who spent many years in the African jungles observing the life and behavior of the chimpanzee. Through lengthy observation she was able to describe the behavior of wild chimps and devise generalities regarding their behavior patterns. The classical field method does not attempt to create situations for an organism to respond to; rather, it permits the discovery of natural laws by observation of naturally occurring phenomena.

The *laboratory method* rests on the ability of a scientist to manipulate some facet of the environment and to measure the result of this manipulation. Scientists control, as much as possible, all facets of the environment (which are termed *variables*) except the one whose effect they are interested in (called the independent variable). For example, in a laboratory study of mate preferences among domestic dogs, it might be hypothesized that odor is an important variable in determining mate preference. The experimenter would then present male dogs with females differing only in odor—the other variables, such as size, coloration and prior experience, would be the same for all the females. Thus, the experimenter could say what effect the presence of a particular odor (the dependent variable) has on mating preference of male dogs. The scientist has, thus, controlled the variables that the dog is confronted with. *Control* is the distinguishing feature of the laboratory method. Logically, field study should be able to describe behaviors seen in the natural setting and their probable causes, whereas the laboratory method should be able to identify precisely the causes and the effect of their manipulation. In practice, however, scientists do not operate in such prescribed areas; rather, they employ both methods in their search for laws of nature. In fact field study is often a prelude to laboratory investigation.

In the study of behavior, these two methods are emphasized to varying degrees by different groups of scientists. Historically, *ethologists,* primarily European and trained as zoologists, have tended to emphasize the field approach. The laboratory method was emphasized by American scientists who are generally psychologists by training. Today, this distinction is little evident and both approaches are used complementarily one to the other.

===== Summary
====

===== *In this section we have seen that we are all students of behavior. We all analyze, criticize and complement one another's behavior every day. However, our views of the behavior of others are slanted; they are biased by our prejudices and by our incomplete understanding of situations. Scientific study of behavior attempts to do away with prejudices and biases. One of the critical elements of the scientific investigation of behavior is controlling variables that might affect and influence an experiment. Methods of limiting the genetic and experimental differences among subjects in an experiment were discussed. There are two basic methods of scientific investigation. In the field method organisms are observed in "the wild" where they can behave in their natural habitat, unhampered by the restrictions of a laboratory environment. However, variables cannot be controlled very effectively in the field, and thus when a precise examination of one variable is desired, the laboratory method is often chosen. The most important feature of the laboratory method is the incorporation of controls.*

Suggestions for Further Reading

Many of the *Scientific American* articles included among these suggestions are available as separate off-prints, which may be ordered by number from Scientific American, % W. H. Freeman and Company, 41 Madison Avenue, New York, New York 10010.

Agranoff, B. W. "Memory and Protein Synthesis." *Scientific American,* June 1967. (Offprint 1077)

DiCara, L. V. "Learning in the Autonomic Nervous System." *Scientific American,* January 1970. (Offprint 525)

Eisner, T., and Wilson, E. O. *Animal Behavior.* San Francisco: W. H. Freeman, 1975.

Gerard, R. W. "What Is Memory?" *Scientific American,* September 1953. (Offprint 11)

Hockett, C. F. "The Origin of Speech." *Scientific American,* September 1960. (Offprint 603)

Kandel, E. R., and Schwartz, J. H. "Molecular biology of learning: Modulation of transmitter release." *Science,* 218 (1982), pp. 433–442.

Lorenz, K. Z. "The Evolution of Behavior." *Scientific American,* December 1958. (Offprint 412)

Luria, A. R. "The Functional Organization of the Brain." *Scientific American,* March 1970. (Offprint 526)

Morris, D. *The Naked Ape.* New York: McGraw-Hill, 1967.

Premack, A. J., and Premack, D. "Teaching Language to an Ape." *Scientific American,* October 1972. (Offprint 549)

Pribram, K. H. "The Neurophysiology of Remembering." *Scientific American,* January 1969. (Offprint 520)

Skinner, B. F. "How to Teach Animals." *Scientific American,* December 1951. (Offprint 423)

Tinbergen, N. "The Curious Behavior of the Stickleback." *Scientific American,* December 1952. (Offprint 414)

Topoff, H. *Animal Societies and Evolution.* San Francisco: W. H. Freeman, 1981.

Wittenberger, J. F. *Animal Social Behavior.* Boston: Duxbury Press, 1981.

2
Biological
Bases of
Behavior

Behavior as Movement

All behavior is the result of muscle movement or glandular secretion. Try to imagine a behavior expressed via any other means. You cannot. Muscles and to a lesser extent, glands, are controlled primarily by the nervous system. Without the involvement of each of these components, behavior would not exist. As our main "behavioral output" proceeds from the muscular system, we shall examine it briefly.

The basic function of any muscle is to contract. Skeletal muscles are attached to the bony skeleton by tough tendons and move the skeleton by contracting. A muscle can only contract or pull; it cannot push. Therefore, a reversal in the direction of a movement of the arm, for example, must come about by the contraction of a second set of muscles. As a moment's reflection will confirm, most muscles in the human body exist in pairs—termed extensors and flexors (Figure 6). These functional groups of muscles work in a highly coordinated manner,

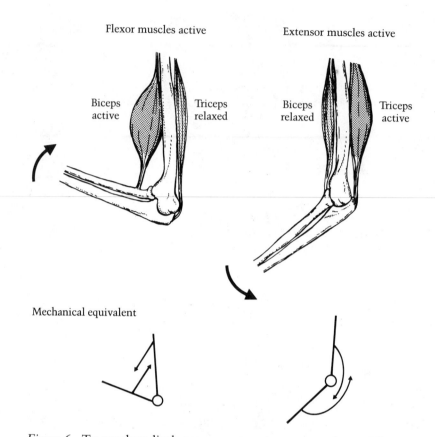

Flexor muscles active   Extensor muscles active

Biceps   Triceps   Biceps   Triceps
active   relaxed   relaxed   active

Mechanical equivalent

Figure 6 To produce limb movement, extensor muscles and flexor muscles must work together cooperatively. To produce forearm flexion the biceps muscles must contract and the triceps muscles must relax. Forearm extension calls for triceps contraction and biceps relaxation. When both are equally contracted (as in isometric exercises), they counteract each other and no movement results.

yet are antagonistic, that is, they produce opposite results. Proponents of isometric exercises take advantage of the antagonistic nature of muscles and base an exercise program on the simultaneous activation of flexors and extensors—the end result is no movement, but considerable expenditure of energy.

A muscle, such as the biceps of your upper arm, consists of many small cylindrical fibers, each capable of independent contraction. Peering at a muscle fiber under the extremely high magnification of the electron microscope, the observer is struck by the orderly geometric pattern and the presence of tiny tubes within the fiber. These tiny tubes, the *myofibrils* (literally meaning "muscle fibrils"), are only a micrometer in diameter (one micrometer is 1/1,000,000 of a meter or 1/25,000 of an inch). The myofibrils are built of two proteins. During muscular contraction the two proteins slide past one another, resulting in a shortening of the myofibril (Figure 7).

Muscular contraction and thus most behavior is based on untold trillions of protein molecules sliding past one another. Muscles do not operate by themselves; they

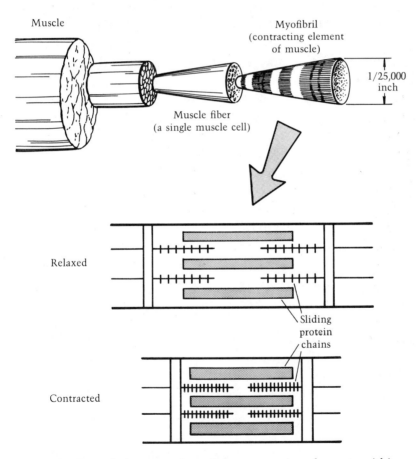

Figure 7 An artist's conception of the contracting elements within a muscle. The myofibril contains two different kinds of protein chains that, when the muscle is activated, slide past one another resulting in the contraction of the muscle.

require input from the nervous system to provoke contraction (although some muscles, such as the smooth muscle of the intestine and the heart muscle, can contract rhythmically in the absence of neural input). The nervous system influences muscle by messages sent along nerves.

The building block of the nervous system is the nerve cell, or *neuron*. The *cell bodies* are enlarged regions of neurons that contain the nuclei and usually lie within the brain or the spinal cord. A *nerve* comprises the long extensions (called *axons*) of many neurons. The nerve supplying a limb muscle, for example, has its origin in the spinal cord (Figure 8). It is only the axon that makes the lengthy journey from the cell body to a muscle; a nerve is thus a bundle of axons. The neuron causes the muscle to contract by means of a chemical released from the end of the axon. This chemical transmits the message calling for contraction from nerve to muscle. This chemical transmitter acts on the muscle to cause the proteins to slide past one another. In the muscle, the neurotransmitter is the chemical *acetylcholine*.

A spinal cord neuron does not have much of "a mind of its own" and thus must in turn rely on other parts of the nervous system for most commands to contract the muscle it controls. The spinal cord is, however, rather good at such simple jobs as reflex reactions to stimuli. Common reflexes, such as the knee jerk or the scratch reflex of a dog, are examples of spinal reflexes that do not rely on brain signals. Some spinal reflexes are so quick and so automatic that they occur before the brain even perceives the stimulus. For example, a withdrawal reflex to a painful stimulus actually occurs before the perception of the pain.

===== Summary

===== *In this short section we have seen that the behavior of animals is expressed by their muscles. We have come to understand a bit of the operation of the muscles and of the controlling*

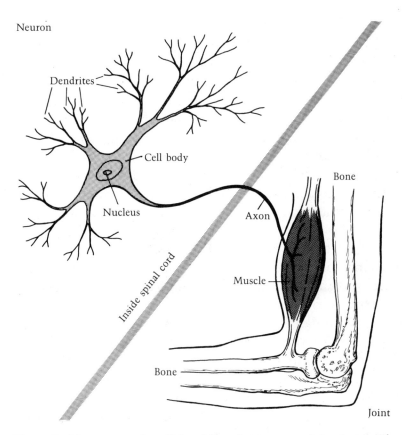

Figure 8 Nerve–muscle relationships. A neuron, originating inside the spinal cord, communicates with the muscle by means of a long axon. The axon thus is the output end of the neuron. Input to the neuron arrives via the dendrites and the cell body.

influences that direct the muscles. A good deal is known about the structure of the muscle and how it works, even down to the chemical basis of contraction which ultimately entails the action of proteins sliding past one another. A nerve supplying a muscle has its origin in the spinal cord or brain and communicates with the muscle by its constituent long processes—the axons. The neuron transmits a message down its axon, releasing a chemical at the end that causes the muscle to contract.

The Neuron as Gland

We have seen that muscles are controlled by chemical substances, termed *transmitters,* which are released from neurons. Actually, the entire nervous system works in the same way—by the release of a chemical transmitter from the terminal of an axon that, in this case, has an effect on another neuron rather than on a muscle. The transmitters are manufactured in the cell body and travel down the long axon to accumulate in tiny packets for later release or are assembled at the site of release in the axon terminal.

The cell body contains many structures necessary to the continued health and well-being of the cell. The most prominent structure, the nucleus, contains the genetic information required to build the cell. The genetic material is deoxyribonucleic acid (DNA). In fact, the DNA within any nucleus carries enough genetic information to specify the building of an entire organism. This fact has led biologists to attempt to recreate an individual organism from a single cell. To date, these efforts, known as *cloning,* have been successful with plants and frogs. In cloning, the DNA is removed from the cell of a mature organism and placed into an egg cell of another organism. The transplanted DNA contains the genetic information required to "build" an organism identical to the donor. By placing the DNA of ten cells from a single frog into ten host egg cells, ten frogs identical to the donor can be produced. If it becomes possible to clone human tissues, the possibilities for producing organs and limbs for those suffering from injury or disease will have a major impact on medicine. Biologists may well have to consider other aspects of cloning humans. Scores of Einsteins are a far different matter from scores of Hitlers!

While it is not currently possible to clone human tissues, it is possible to take isolated normal segments of DNA and insert "foreign" DNA into them, such that the DNA will then produce whatever it was that the spliced-in segment codes for. Since DNA codes for the production of proteins which serve as the body's structural elements, enzymes and cellular machines, it is possible to produce a novel protein by splicing a segment of DNA into an existing DNA strand. The new protein, one that is not normally produced by the original strand of DNA, can then be extracted and put to use in medicine and industry.

These techniques, known as recombinant DNA techniques, are currently being used to produce extremely rare and valuable molecules that cannot be synthesized in the laboratory. Examples of the use of recombinant DNA techniques in medicine include such valuable molecules as insulin, growth hormone, interferon and many others. In industry, recombinant techniques are being used to alter bacteria so that they will be capable of cleaning up oil spills and toxic wastes. In essence, the recombinant DNA procedure makes tiny factories out of bacteria to produce useful molecules which can then be used for human purposes.

There are unique proteins found in the brain. We do not know what most of these proteins do. When their function is discovered, however, it may be that some of them are involved in mental health, learning, memory, the maintainance of body weight or heretofore unsuspected roles. If these proteins turn out to be useful, it is almost a certainty that recombinant DNA techniques will be utilized to manufacture them for administration to needy humans.

The cytoplasm surrounding the nucleus contains several other specialized structures; among them are ribosomes (sites of protein manufacture), golgi bodies (probable site of transmitter manufacture) and mitochondria (sites of conversion of glucose or blood sugar and oxygen into cellular energy). A complex network of minute tubes interlaces the cytoplasm, extending into the fine extensions of the neuron. These tubes are thought to transport materials within the cell. A membrane surrounds the cytoplasm. The structure of the membrane is such that it allows certain material to pass into or out of the cytoplasm. This selective passage of materials is essential to cellular metabolism and excretion in general and for the operation of the nervous system.

Several other fine extensions of the neuron, in addition to the axon, are shown in Figure 8, and these are finely branched. They are *dendrites*. Just as axons carry "messages" away from the cell body, the dendrites convey information to the cell body. Contacts coming from other neurons are made primarily on the dendrites and secondarily on the cell body itself; contacts are infrequently made on the axon. Thus, incoming information travels via dendrites, and outgoing information via axons. We have been using the word *contacts* to describe the communication between two neurons. To be accurate, the neurons do not actually touch; rather, there is an almost infinitesimally small (1/50,000,000 of a meter) gap between the axon of one and the dendrite (or cell body) of another. This gap is called the *synaptic gap;* the term *synapse* refers to the synaptic gap and the adjoining axonal and dendritic membranes. The transmitter is released from storage packets in the end of the axon into the synapse where it has an effect on the opposing dendrite or cell body. A transmitter released by the axon of a neuron can do one of two things: it may arouse (excite) or it may depress (inhibit) the action of the adjoining neuron (Figure 9).

Since there are two primary actions of transmitters—excitation or inhibition—it may come as a surprise that there exist 15 or 20 different kinds of neurotransmitters in the body. The reasons for so many different kinds of neurotransmitters are not completely understood. It is thought, however, that specific brain systems may have developed particular neurotransmitters to accomplish their purposes. For example, the neurotransmitter *serotonin* has been implicated in brain control of sleep and wakefulness, whereas the neurotransmitters *dopamine* and *norepinephrine* have been implicated in mental disorders, mood and emotionality. In addition to the neurotransmitters, which generally have an immediate effect on the cells they influence, there are agents in the brain that act to modulate the activ-

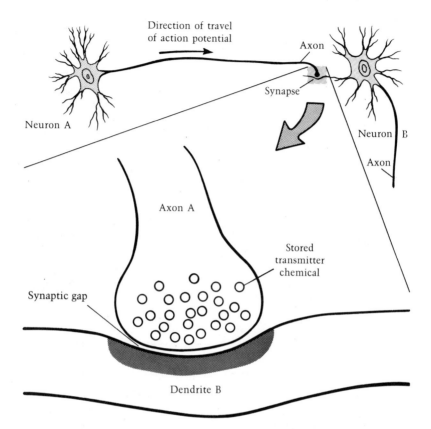

Figure 9 Synapse. Neuron A communicates with Neuron B via a synapse between an axon and a dendrite. The expanded part of the illustration shows the synaptic gap, which is actually a tiny space separating the membranes of the two neurons. Transmitter chemical stored in tiny packets in the axon is released into the synaptic gap upon the arrival of an action potential. The transmitter chemical then either excites or inhibits the activity of Neuron B.

ity of neurotransmitters. Still other agents act as brain hormones, influencing widespread brain regions. We are just learning about these neuromodulators and neurohormones and the roles they play in regulating brain and behavioral processes.

Most of the neurotransmitters and neuromodulators act on the cells that they affect by binding to a *receptor* protein on the surface of the cell. The receptor will only bind molecules that have certain complementary shapes

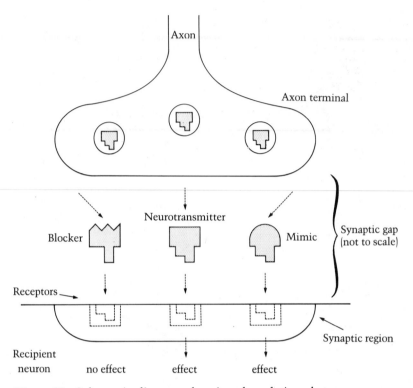

Figure 10 Schematic diagram showing the relations between a neurotransmitter and its receptor. Based largely on complementary shape and electric charge, the neurotransmitter fits its receptor much as a key fits a lock. The normal effect of the neurotransmitter can be mimicked by drugs sharing these shape and charge properties. A blocker drug has sufficient similarities to bind to the receptor, but often does not trigger the effect. Since it occupies the receptor, it prevents (or blocks) the neurotransmitter from having its normal effect.

(Figure 10). When the neurotransmitter or neuromodulator binds to the receptor, it stimulates a response from the cell. The response might be excitatory or inhibitory or one that modulates the effectiveness of other synaptic inputs. Although it is customary to refer to excitatory or inhibitory neurotransmitters, the nature of the response depends on the properties of the receptor molecule. This feature of synaptic transmission, relying on specific receptors to neurotransmitters, allows us to introduce foreign chemicals into the brain which can also bind to these receptors.

Foreign chemicals which have the capacity of binding to receptors can act in basically two ways. First, they may mimic the natural neurotransmitter and trigger a response by the cell. Alternatively, they may bind to the receptor but fail to trigger the response in the cell. In so doing they also prevent natural neurotransmitters from binding to the receptor. The latter class of drugs are termed, thus, blockers. As an example of the former class of drugs—that is, a drug that mimics the operation of a naturally occurring neurotransmitter—is the drug L-DOPA. L-DOPA is a precursor of the naturally occurring neurotransmitter, dopamine. L-DOPA is given to patients suffering from a disease that selectively destroys dopamine-producing neurons. Thus these patients suffer from a lack of dopamine. The administration of L-DOPA acts to increase the brain levels of dopamine. There are many drugs that act as blockers of particular neurotransmitter systems. Many of the drugs used for the treatment of psychotic illness are effective dopamine blockers. These drugs include the chlorpromazines and haloperidol.

Once a neurotransmitter molecule binds to a receptor molecule, it must be inactivated so that information may again be transmitted through that synapse. Most neurotransmitters are deactivated by a reuptake process wherein they are taken back into the axon terminal from where they arose. Some drugs, such as cocaine and amphetamines, act by interfering with the reuptake mechanism. The net effect of interfering with the reuptake of a neurotransmitter is to leave more of it in the region of the synapse and thus, make more of it available for binding with receptors. Thus, the net effect of a drug that interferes with reuptake is to act as if one had an excess of neurotransmitter in the synapse. While the pharmacology of synaptic transmission is considerably more complicated than outlined above, and while drugs are available that affect nearly all aspects of synaptic chemistry, the intent here is to emphasize that most of the drugs that influence the brain, including drugs of abuse, do so by acting at the receptors for neurotransmitters and neuromodulators.

Unfortunately for drug users, there are consequences to the long-term use of psychoactive drugs. For instance, in the presence of a mimic, the synthesis of the normal neurotransmitter molecule may shut down. When the drug is no longer used, there may be insufficient amounts of the natural neurotransmitter molecule present, causing severe withdrawal symptoms. This is what occurs during withdrawal from morphine addiction—a topic we shall consider in more detail later in this book.

Transmitter is released when a nerve impulse arrives at the end of the axon. We measure the nerve impulse as a change in voltage moving down the axon at speeds of up to 100 meters per second (which is far short of the speed of electricity—namely, 300,000,000 meters per second). The voltage, however, is merely a convenient by-product of the nerve impulse: "convenient" in that it can be recorded and measured by scientists. The nerve impulse itself, usually called an *action potential,* is a transient alteration in the cell membrane that allows a brief flow of ions (electrically charged chemical components of cytoplasm) across it. The "potential" in the term is short for *potential difference*—the electric charge of some point relative to the electric charge of some other point. The action potential travels down the axon to release transmitter at the terminal of the axon. The action potential has been compared to a fuse used on explosives. Once lit it will burn at a constant rate down the length of the fuse. Although a burning fuse is like an axon in that the changes in both are chemical reactions, the axon can be "used" again and again (that is, it is a regenerative process) whereas a fuse can be burned only once.

A neuron will "fire" (conduct an action potential down its axon) when the cell body has been sufficiently aroused or excited by the input it receives. As a cell receives both excitatory and inhibitory input, often simultaneously, it will fire only when the excitatory transmitter input exceeds by a critical amount the inhibitory transmitter input. Once the critical amount is reached, there is an action potential (Figure 11).

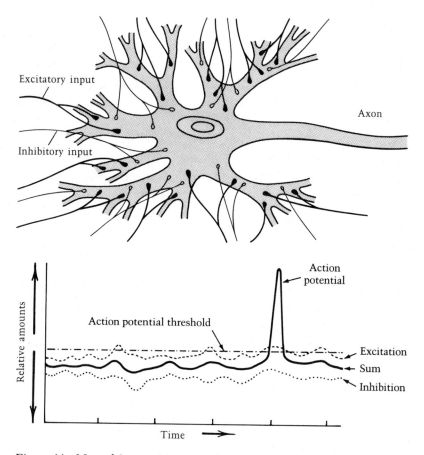

Figure 11 Neural input. Most neurons receive input from both excitatory and inhibitory sources. Whether an action potential is produced in a neuron at any particular moment depends largely upon the relative excitation and inhibition. Only when excitation exceeds inhibition by a sufficient amount is an action potential generated.

Thus, each of our more than 100 billion neurons has several kinds of input that together determine whether it will fire, and each of these neurons communicates with about 1,000 other cells. All of this is the more amazing when we realize that all behaviors, thoughts and feelings are the result of the relations between individual neurons multiplied millions, or even billions, of times. Indeed, the tremendous mass of minutiae that we remember and carry with us is also laid down and read out, if not stored, in this elementary manner. It is somewhat surprising, considering their awesome task, that we are not capable of replacing neurons that have died. Once lost, they are not regenerated. This is one of the factors producing senility in old age. Counteracting this is the continuous elaboration of the dendrites of mature neurons. This latter observation suggests that neurons may have the ability to grow new synapses throughout life—indeed, this is theorized to occur as a means of storing memory in the brain, but we shall cover this topic in more detail later.

===== Summary

===== *It is hoped that the title of this section Neuron as Gland is now clear. For, in a very real sense, it is perfectly acceptable to view each individual neuron as a secreting gland whose product (the transmitter molecule) plays a specific role (initiation of an action potential) analogous to the product of the salivary gland whose specific role in the first stages of digestion is to secrete salivary fluid into the mouth.*

A neuron is like any other cell in the body in that it needs to receive oxygen and food, and eliminate waste products. In addition, it is specialized for the transmission of information; it transmits information by means of specialized parts of the cell, dendrites and axons, and by specialized contacts between cells: the synapses. We have seen how neurons can have either excitatory or inhibitory effects on adjacent cells, and how the net result of excitation or inhibition may be the production of an action potential that, upon arrival at the end of an axon, releases a chemical transmitter that either excites or inhibits the next cell in line. In a real sense, then, the neuron is a tiny secreting gland.

===== ***Collections of Neurons***

===== The brain of any complicated organism (and of quite a few rather uncomplicated ones) is considerably more than a loose collection of neurons. The brain is highly organized and specialized. By way of analogy, a large corporation is composed of many departments, such as personnel, purchasing, shipping and executive. Each department has a specific job to do, and a chart may be drawn of the organization showing lines of command and communication. Many scientists believe this is also true of the brain. There are departments concerned with decoding information about the world. Other departments process the information and arrive at "executive decisions" regarding a course of action, and still other departments function to set the muscles of the organism into operation. One of the goals of the neurosciences is to identify the "departments" within the brain and their "lines of command." As in an efficient corporation, work is accomplished only by the interaction and cooperation of many elements.

Perhaps the best way to understand the incredibly complex puzzle presented by the numerous specialized regions of the brain and the interconnections among them is to understand something of the development of the brain. We can view this development from two perspectives: by observing changes in an individual brain from conception to maturity or by comparing the human brain with those of progressively simpler organisms. Drawings of the developing human brain in a few embryological stages (Figure 12) show some basic structures: the spinal cord, the brainstem and the forebrain. These basic structures of the brain are elaborated, enlarged, and in some animals, engulfed during development. The brainstem, for example, is very much overshadowed by the various forebrain structures in the developing human brain. In fact, as will be seen below, the tremendous development of the forebrain is a feature crucial in making humans what they are.

Now consider the brains of simpler organisms in relation to the human brain (Figure 13). As we examine simple (fish) to complex (cat) brains, we note that the forebrain becomes tremendously enlarged relative to the other areas of the brain.

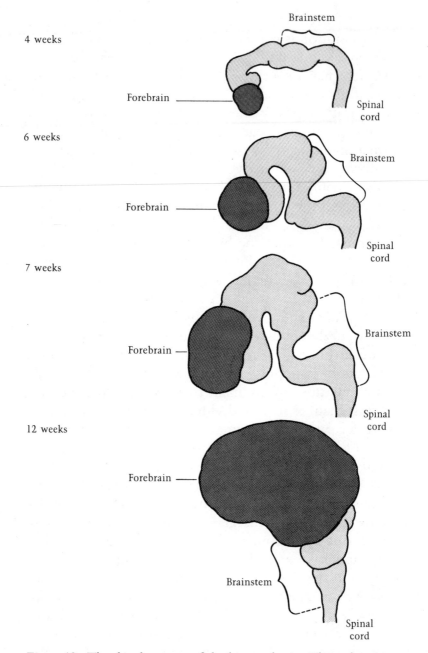

Figure 12 The development of the human brain. These drawings (not to scale) made from human embryos of ages noted, show the development of three of the basic neural structures in the brain.

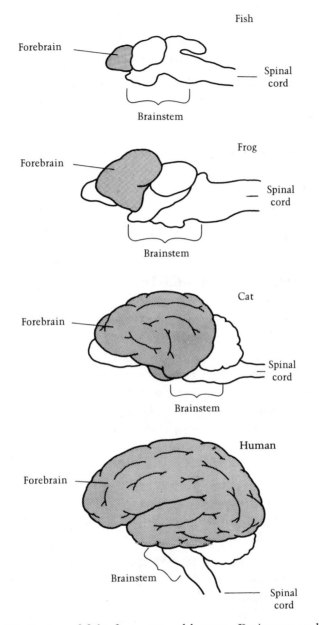

Figure 13 Brains of fish, frog, cat and human. Brainstem and spinal cord structures are relatively similar in all four species. As development proceeded from fish to human, the forebrain became tremendously enlarged, eventually engulfing the brainstem. (The drawings are not to scale.)

As we have said, the brain is not an amorphous mass of tissue; rather, it is composed of interrelated components. We shall briefly identify and outline the functions of the major of these brain divisions. Basically, your nervous system, like that of the fish, bird and cat, consists of a concentrated mass of neural tissue (the *central nervous system,* which includes the brain and spinal cord) and a widely distributed system of nerves and sensory receptors (the *peripheral nervous system*).

Peripheral Nervous System

The peripheral nervous system consists of the nerves connecting skin, muscles and various organs to the brain. These nerves carry sensory information about the body and the external world to the brain. The nerves of the peripheral nervous system also carry motor commands to the muscles, glands and organs of the body. Actually, the peripheral nervous system performs two quite different jobs, and it is thus subdivided into two systems. One type of function is related to keeping all the internal machinery of the body working properly and making adjustments for changing demands upon the body. The nerves having this type of function, which supply the heart, kidney, liver, gastrointestinal tract and circulatory system of the body, operate very much on their own—we generally do not pay much attention to our heart rate or blood pressure (unless we are hypochondriacs), yet the system is continuously changing to accommodate the demands the central nervous system puts upon it.

For instance, when we run up a flight of stairs, our heart rate increases and the blood flow to our muscles increases to supply them with oxygen, yet we are generally unaware of these changes—until, that is, we arrive at the top of the stairs with our heart pounding. This subdivision of the peripheral nervous system is termed the *auto-*

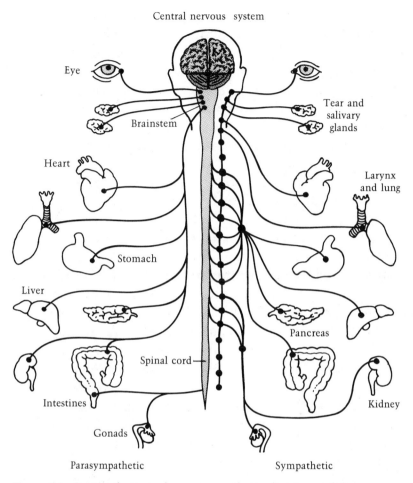

Central nervous system

Eye

Brainstem

Tear and salivary glands

Heart

Larynx and lung

Stomach

Liver

Pancreas

Spinal cord

Intestines

Kidney

Gonads

Parasympathetic

Sympathetic

Figure 14 Sympathetic and parasympathetic divisions of the autonomic nervous system and the organs that they innervate. Only half of each division of the autonomic nervous system is shown. Both divisions supply organs on both sides of the body.

nomic nervous system (Figure 14). Students occasionally misread *autonomic* and come up with "automatic nervous system," which would not be a bad name as the system operates with little conscious help from us. It should be emphasized that simply because we, as members of Western society, cannot modify at will the actions of the autonomic nervous system, it does not follow that it is impossible to do so. Some Eastern societies, which emphasize introspection more than most Western societies, can provide examples of persons capable of altering their autonomic functions at will. You have, no doubt, heard of individuals who claim to be able to slow their hearts, walk on hot embers or stick pins through their skin without pain or bleeding. These persons have learned how to modify autonomic functions.

The autonomic nervous system works very much like the accelerator and the brake on an automobile. Part of it works to increase heart rate, blood flow or other vital functions, and part to decrease heart rate and blood flow. In the autonomic nervous system, however, often both the "accelerator" and the "brake" are being applied at the same time. Now, if we were to drive an automobile in this manner (and some people do!), speed (or whether there were any motion at all) would depend on the relative force applied to the accelerator and the brake. In the autonomic nervous system, the "accelerator" is termed the *sympathetic division* and the "brake" is the *parasympathetic division.* Generally, both are operative, but one or the other is predominant. Historically, it has been thought that the sympathetic functions to mobilize overall bodily resources for action. The parasympathetic functions to conserve and maintain specific bodily resources. While this may be an oversimplification, it does capture the essence of the functioning of the autonomic nervous system.

The other subdivision of the peripheral nervous system, called the *somatic nervous system,* is responsible for what we usually call "behavior." That is, messages for movements are conveyed by this part of the peripheral nervous system from the brain to muscle, and sensations are conveyed by it from sense organ receptors to the brain. The somatic nervous system, like the autonomic, consists of both sensory and motor nerves, and *unlike* the autonomic nervous system, is more or less under our conscious control.

Central Nervous System

The central nervous system can be conveniently divided into three parts: spinal cord, brainstem and forebrain. The brainstem and forebrain can each be further subdivided into several functional groups. In the sections below each of the major parts and their subdivisions will be discussed.

The Brain as a Walnut

To understand the design of the brain, you might find it useful to consider an analogy: Picture, if you will, a walnut—in its shell. The meat of the walnut is protected inside a tough shell, much the same as our delicate brain is surrounded by a bony, protective skull. The meat of the walnut is covered by a thin, tightly adhering membrane, just as the brain is covered by several such membranes, called _meninges_. These membranes, three in number, have fluid between them and act as "shock absorbers" for the brain.

A cursory inspection of the nutmeat shows it to consist of two very wrinkled halves connected by a stalk. If the surface area of the wrinkled nutmeat were to be compared with that of a ball of the same diameter, that of the nutmeat would be many times greater than that of the ball. The brain also is constructed of two halves, or hemispheres, that are connected by neural tissue. The outer surface of the brain (the neocortex) is wrinkled or convoluted, just like that of the walnut.

The analogy between a walnut and the human brain is hardly a new idea. In the seventeenth century the English herbalist William Coles wrote, "Walnuts have the perfect signature of the head: the outer husk or green covering represents the Pericranium or outward skin of the skull, whereon the hair groweth, and therefore salts made of those husks or barks are exceedingly good for wounds in the head. The inner woody shell hath the signature of the skull and the little yellow skin or fell that covers the kernel of the hard Meninga and Pia-Mater, which are the thin surfaces which envelop the brain. The kernel hath the very figure of the brain, and therefore it is very preferable for the brain and resists poisons; for if the kernel be bruised and moistened with the quintescence of wine, and laid upon the crown of the head, it comforts the brain and head mightily." From the Middle Ages through Coles' day, the resemblance had been taken to be God's indication for man's benefit that the walnut was medicine for ills of the brain. If today we are no longer able to believe in such curative powers, we can, nevertheless, put the walnut to use as a physical model of the brain.

Spinal cord The human *spinal cord* is about the diameter of your little finger and is primarily responsible for the routing of commands between the brain and the body. The other major tasks of the spinal cord are to direct various coordinating reflexes and to protect the body from tissue damage by withdrawal reflexes of various sorts. Examples include the knee-jerk reflex and the withdrawal reflex elicited by placing your hand on a hot stove. Reflexive behavior is controlled by the spinal cord without the direct participation of the brain. Considering the rather crucial nature of its job, it is not surprising that the spinal cord is afforded a considerable amount of protection. A fluid-filled sack inside the vertebrae encases the spinal cord, and acts as a "shock absorber." The brain is similarly protected inside the skull. A parallel principle is at work in protecting a developing human in the womb of its mother.

The spinal cord is encased in a bony skeleton, the *vertebrae,* which offers considerable mechanical support and protection. Nevertheless, occasionally the protective devices are overstrained, resulting in a break in the spinal cord. When this occurs, the region of the body below the break is both anesthetic (without feeling) and paralyzed. If the spinal cord is not extensively damaged in the break, then the paralyzed area will and does respond on a reflexive level, although the victim may not be aware of the actions of his or her limbs because of the anesthesia.

The spinal cord is a relatively simple part of the central nervous system, yet it contains the basic cell types found in the brain itself. Because of this, it has proved to be a valuable tool or "model" of the more complex brain. Cell types found in the brain and the spinal cord are: (1) *sensory neurons*—cells concerned with bringing information into the central nervous system; (2) *interneurons*—cells whose job is to process information between input and output; and (3) *motor neurons*—cells that receive information from either sensory neurons or interneurons and in turn project to the output apparatus—muscle or gland (Figure 15).

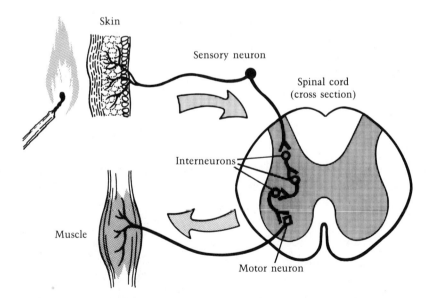

Figure 15 Sensations on the surface of the skin conducted into the spinal cord by a sensory neuron. Numerous interneurons relay the information to a motor neuron that when activated causes a muscle to contract. This simple reflex arc protects us from damaging stimuli. Note that the participation of the brain is not required.

The human brain is composed, basically, of these three cell types, with interneurons far outnumbering the other two. A brain interneuron is not much different from a spinal cord interneuron, nor, for that matter is a human interneuron much different from a salamander interneuron. It is quite true that we can view human attributes not as the consequence of having a brain, which all complex organisms have, nor of simply possessing interneurons, but of having a brain that consists of many more interneurons with much more intricate interconnections than any other species (except perhaps dolphins and whales).

Brainstem   The *brainstem* refers to a collection of structures located at the base of the brain. Brainstem structures are very similar across a wide range of organisms. As relatively simple animals have these structures, the functions of these brain areas are probably relatively basic. A posterior portion of the brainstem contains areas whose function is to regulate heart rate, blood pressure, respiration, and stomach and intestinal contraction. These areas are associated with the autonomic nervous system. Also found in the posterior brainstem are various sensory and motor axons that extend into the spinal cord.

Reticular formation   Ascending through the brainstem is a structure whose discovery made a major impact on the brain sciences in the 1940s. The *reticular formation* is a diffuse collection of neurons found in the core of the brainstem and projecting from the spinal cord into the *cortex*. Most incoming sensory information is routed to the reticular formation in addition to projecting to the specific sensory decoding areas on the cortex. Research indicates that the reticular formation, from which axons go out to all parts of the cortex, functions to alert or focus the attention of an organism (Figure 16). It is the activity in the reticular formation of your pet cat that leads it to come running from a considerable distance at the sound of the can opener, a stimulus that has great significance to the cat.

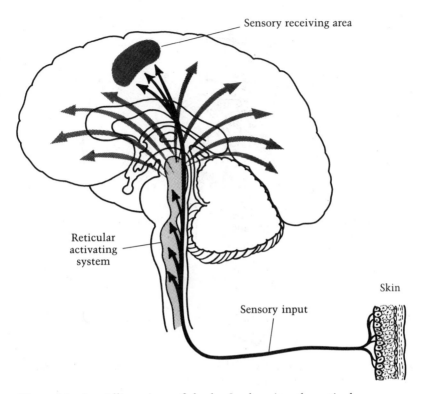

Figure 16 A midline view of the brain showing the reticular activating system. Sensory information coming into the brain influences the reticular activating system so that the entire forebrain is aroused. In addition, specific sensory information is routed to the appropriate cortical sensory area. (Adapted from "The Reticular Formation" by J. D. French. Copyright 1957 by Scientific American, Inc. All rights reserved.)

Most anesthetics and tranquilizers inhibit this brainstem structure.

Cerebellum Overlying the brainstem is another structure that is changed little across species—the *cerebellum* (Figure 17). It has been known for centuries that the cerebellum has something to do with the coordination of movement, yet the means by which it operated was unknown. Recently, scientists have gained considerable insight into the "wiring diagram" of the cerebellum. The cerebellum con-

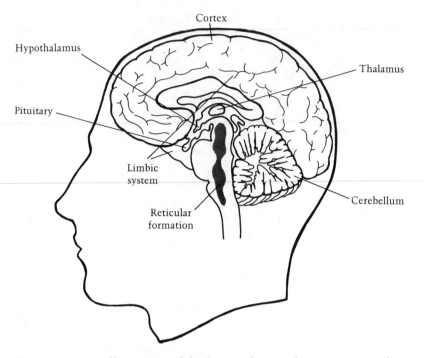

Figure 17 A midline view of the human brain. Shown are several of the structures referred to in the text.

sists of a wrinkled sheet of cells on the outer surface and nuclei deep within the cerebellum. The cerebellum receives information from widespread areas of the spinal cord and brain and, in turn, projects to motor areas of the brain to modulate movement. As is true in most scientific endeavors in which something is investigated more and more closely, the picture may become more and more complex. Yet we can hope that the recent discoveries regarding the organization and function of the cerebellum and adjacent structures foreshadow significant breakthroughs in our understanding of brain function. For example, Richard Thompson at Stanford University has discovered that the cerebellum is involved in an animal's learning of a simple eye-blink movement. Lesions to certain regions of the cerebellum selectively impair the learned response, not affecting unlearned responses.

Forebrain   The greatest bulk of the human brain is the <u>forebrain</u>. This portion of the central nervous system finds its greatest elaboration in humans. The forebrain consists of the thalamus, hypothalamus and pituitary, limbic system and neocortex (see Fig. 17). Each of these areas will be discussed below.

Thalamus   The incoming sensory information that was seen to pass by way of the reticular formation finds its way to the <u>thalamus</u>. The thalamus consists of a large number of nuclei (specialized collections of neurons—not to be confused with the nucleus of the cell) whose job entails the relaying of sensory information to the appropriate areas of the neocortex. The incoming sensory information is then further processed in the neocortex, as we shall see later. The thalamus also receives information sent down from the neocortex. In the thalamus, specific areas are associated with the different forms of sensory information—vision, hearing, touch and so forth. This brain structure is indispensable to the human species, for without it we would be incapable of vision, hearing or feeling.

   A quite different function is served by a collection of thalamic areas that receives information from a wide variety of sources. These nonspecific areas have axons going up to the neocortex as well as to other places. Unlike the sensory-specific relay nuclei, they have axons spreading through the entirety of the neocortex rather than limiting their output to the specific neocortical sensory areas. The function of this nonspecific part of the thalamus appears to parallel the functions of the reticular formation. Thus, it is involved in alerting or arousing the rest of the brain, and hence the organism, into a state of focused attention on a relevant event in the environment. This area also plays an important role in the processes of sleep and wakefulness.

Hypothalamus   If we were ever to undertake a search for the functional "center of the brain," the logical candidate would have to be the *hypothalamus*. It is a tiny structure buried in the base of the brain. It, like the thalamus, is composed of many nuclei, and each nucleus of the hypothalamus has a specific duty. There are nuclei associated with eating, drinking, sexual behavior, body temperature and fluid balance, sleeping, waking, and in general, emotional behavior of various sorts. An organism deprived of its hypothalamus is incapable of regulating these activities and soon dies.

Pituitary   The hypothalamus, besides having the duties listed above, is also quite intimately associated with the master gland of the body—the *pituitary*. The pituitary lies immediately below the hypothalamus, and a thin stalk of tissue connects the two: Thus, brain (hypothalamus) meets gland (pituitary). The marriage is a happy one, with the functions of brain and gland complementing one another in what is really a single functional system. Our distinctions between muscle and bone, skin and brain, nerve and gland are often creations of our own perspective. The categories into which we sort parts of an organism often do not hold up when examined closely. An example of this is provided by the hypothalamus, a structure considered to be a part of the brain, but which manufactures chemicals (hormones) that are then transported to the pituitary for release into the bloodstream. These hormones regulate the function of many tissues in the body. Among the functions of the hormones are: bodily growth, water retention, control of menstural cycle and sperm production by the gonads and regulation of the functions of many other glands.

Limbic system   The last major region of the brain beneath the cortex is the *limbic system*. As the name implies, it is a collection of many individual structures (including the hippocampus, amygdala, septum) that were historically thought to operate as a single functional system. The limbic system is currently being subjected to concerted study by brain scientists in an attempt to reveal its function. So far our understanding of the limbic system is very incomplete, and arguments ensue even as to whether it should be considered a functional system. However, scientists generally agree that the limbic system appears to be involved in emotionality, motivation and memory.

Neocortex   The human *neocortex* is a wrinkled layer of brain tissue lying immediately beneath the skull and surrounding most of the structures mentioned previously. Of all the cells in the human brain, about three-fourths are found in the neocortex. It is easy to assume from this that the neocortex is performing many tasks that require much neural "machinery." The picture of a large enveloping neocortex does not hold for all organisms, however. Amphibians and fish have no neocortex, and birds and reptiles have only a minute amount. Thus, it is apparent that the neocortex is not necessary to life. In fact, humans suffering from a misfortune of nature are occasionally born lacking a neocortex; their behavior, however, is limited to very primitive responses. As you might guess from the prefix *neo-*, there exists an older variety of cortex as well, some of which is associated with olfaction (the sense of smell) and some of which is associated with the limbic lobe.

Human behavioral characteristics, used in their broadest connotation, are the end product of the activity of the neocortex. What, then, are the functions served by the neocortex?

The neocortical surface is composed of a thin layer of neurons (about as thick as the cover of a hardcover book). In simpler organisms, such as the rat, the neocortex is a smooth covering enveloping the rest of the brain. In primates the smooth neocortical surface has become highly infolded and thus much increased in surface area. It is estimated that at least 60 percent of the surface of the human neocortex is hidden from view in the infolded areas (termed the sulci, as opposed to the "hills," or gyri) (Figure 18).

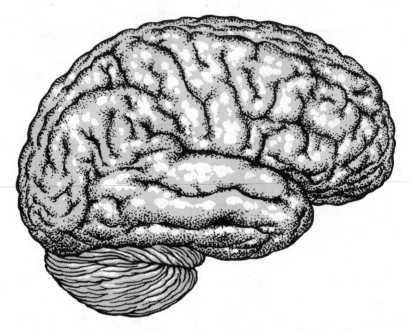

Figure 18 A drawing of the surface of the human brain. The cortex is greatly infolded, with more than half of the surface hidden from view.

Within the neocortex there are numerous subdivisions. The most obvious is that which forms the hemispheres, left and right. Many subcortical structures (those lying under the neocortex) are thus present in the brain as pairs, one in the right hemisphere and one in the left. Each hemisphere is further divided into four lobes, which more or less correspond to major landmarks on the surface of the brain (the lobe names actually refer to the bones of the skull under which they lie). They are the *frontal, parietal, temporal* and *occipital lobes* (Figure 19).

Each of these four lobes contains yet further subdivisions. The parietal, temporal and occipital lobes receive sensory information from "body senses," hearing and vision, respectively. These sensory-receiving areas occupy a small portion of each lobe, the remainder being termed the *association neocortex,* historically thought to be the region where different sensory impressions are registered or asso-

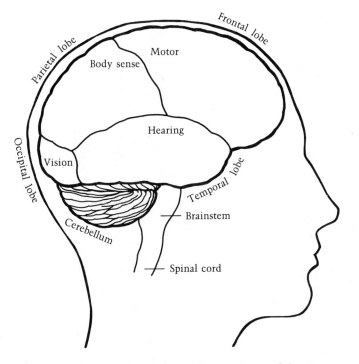

Figure 19 The four lobes of the right hemisphere of the cortex. The left hemisphere is similarly divided into four lobes.

ciated. Each sensory area of the neocortex receives projections primarily from a single sensory organ. That is, the visual-receiving area in the occipital lobe processes sensations received by the retina; the auditory-receiving area in the temporal lobe processes sensation received by the cochlea; and the body-sense-receiving area in the parietal lobe processes sensations received by the body surface. Within each sensory-receiving area, the sense-organ projections form a map of the sensory organ on the neocortical surface. Such a representation is called a *receptortopic* mapping.

To appreciate this organization, consider for a moment the body senses. Touch, pressure, temperature, muscle sense and position sense are included in the body senses. Thus, input from all parts of the body surface (and interior) are represented in this sensory modality. The

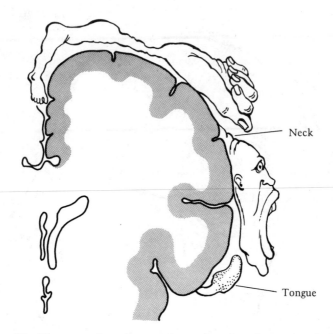

Figure 20 The somatic sensory cortex showing the neocortical representation of various body parts. This is a representation (termed a homunculus) of the left side of the body on the right hemisphere of the brain. The area for a body part is proportional to the sensitivity of that part, thus the enlarged hands and lips.

map on the brain of this information is symbolically represented in Figure 20. An obvious question comes to mind as we look at this illustration: why is the figure so distorted, why are the hands and mouth so exaggerated? The answer is that neocortical area in the brain is allocated in accordance with the fineness of sensation possible. Thus, the parts of our bodies that are the most sensitive are the hands and lips, and they, correspondingly, have a large neocortical area for the processing of their sensations. This distorted neocortical representation is called the *homunculus*. There is a point-to-point representation from a receptor (the retina of the eye, the cochlea of the ear, the surface of the skin) to the specific sensory-receiving area of the neocortex. The amount of neocortical area is proportional to the fineness of discrimination possible. We will come back to this point in our discussion of sensory systems.

For all senses there exist multiple neocortical representations. Stated in another way, there are multiple homunculi for each sense. The multiple representations are all involved in the neocortical processing of sensory information in ways incompletely understood at present. Note from Figure 21 that the sensory and motor pathways of the brain are crossed, that is, most of the sensations from the right hand are registered in the left hemisphere, and a smaller projection is registered on the right hemisphere.

The frontal lobe plays a crucial role in the sending of motor impulses to the muscles via the spinal cord. The motor area, which occupies part of the frontal lobe, is built

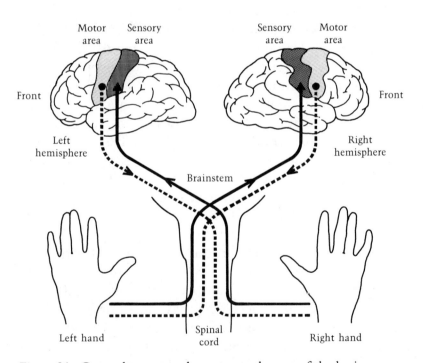

Figure 21 Crossed motor and sensory pathways of the brain. Sensations from the right hand are registered in the left hemisphere; sensations from the left hand are registered in the right hemisphere. This crossed projection is generally true for all sensations. Motor commands to the right hand or leg are similarly generated in the motor area of the left hemisphere. (Adapted from "The Asymmetry of the Human Brain" by D. Kimura. Copyright 1973 by Scientific American, Inc. All rights reserved.)

analogously to the sensory areas. In this case the neocortical surface represents muscles rather than receptors. The strategy is the same—a greater area for parts of the musculature that are capable of fine, precise movement. Thus, the hands and mouth regions here too are disproportionately large. In fact, the body-sense-receiving area (in the parietal lobe) and the motor area (in the frontal lobe), which are physically adjacent, are mirror images of one another.

The sensory and motor areas of the neocortex of humans are rather small compared with the association areas. The association areas probably serve the intricate behavioral responses of which complex organisms are capable. These areas are involved in learning and memory tasks, and as we shall see later, are necessary for the production and understanding of language. Figure 22 depicts the size differences between the brains of several species and the relative amount of neocortical association areas.

Although brain scientists are still trying to delineate the precise function of the association areas, several discoveries have furthered our knowledge of these areas. One of the most exciting discoveries concerns the functions of the speech areas in the dominant hemisphere. (Generally, one hemisphere is dominant—usually the left hemisphere on a right-handed individual.) Portions of the temporal and frontal association areas serve as speech areas—locations that are crucial in the interpretation of language (spoken or written), as well as in the production of language (verbal or written). Humans who, suffering from various kinds of accidents, have lost portions of the speech areas, experience a number of difficulties in interpreting or generating speech (see also page 21). In short, the neocortex is responsible for all higher mental functions and such by-products of the complex interrelations of these functions as society and culture. Without a neocortex, human behavior is reduced to a primitive bundle of reflexes. In Chapter III we shall again consider neocortical functioning.

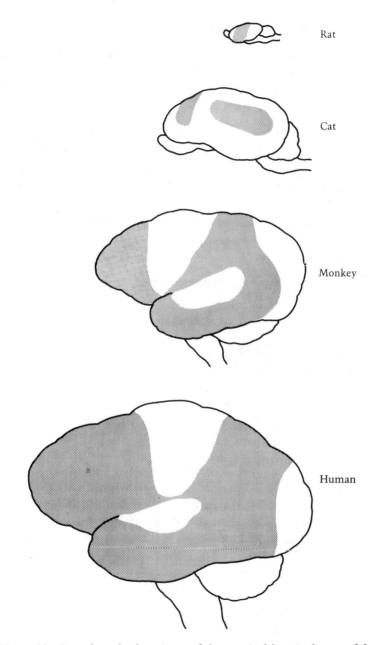

Figure 22 Rough scale drawings of the cortical hemispheres of four mammals. Note both greater size and the relatively larger association cortex (stippled area) in the primates.

Electrical Activity

In a previous section, we discovered that individual neurons in the brain receive input from many different sources. Some of these synaptic inputs are excitatory, others are inhibitory. We have also seen that one of the main functions of a single neuron is to integrate this excitatory and inhibitory information over time, resulting in action potentials if the balance swings far enough toward excitatory. A similar analysis can be applied to collections of neurons. In this section, we have seen that neurons are often found in functional groups. It should come as no surprise then to realize that the electrical activity recorded from any of these collections of neurons will exhibit many of the properties seen within individual neurons.

The vast majority of research concerned with determining the electrical activity of brain regions occurs with laboratory animals because it is necessary to place recording electrodes within the structure of interest. Virtually the only recording done from human beings involves recording the electrical activity of neurons in the neocortex from electrodes pasted to the surface of the scalp. In the animal recordings, it is possible to determine a great deal of the function of a particular brain region by recording the electrical activity elicited when specific stimuli are presented or when specific behaviors are emitted. For example, our knowledge of the organization of cerebral cortex—those regions devoted to the receipt of sensory information and those regions concerned with producing movements—comes from a combination of recording the electrical activity from various points on the cortex while the animal is being subjected to various sensory experiences as well as stimulating portions of the neocortex and watching to see which muscles move.

It may come somewhat as a surprise that there are some regions of the brain whose function remains obscure. Some portions of the limbic system, for example, have been subjected to much analysis including a detailed understanding of their anatomy and recordings of their electrical activity during various behaviors and sensory experiences of the animal. In many cases, the function of a region of brain is also studied by surgically removing or inactivating that region to see what effect it has on the resulting behavior or learning capabilities of the animal. Even in the face of this multipronged attack on the function of these brain regions, there are still numerous instances when the precise role of these brain regions in behavior and bodily functioning is unknown.

≡ Summary

≡ The brain is composed of billions of individual neurons that are gathered together in functional groups. In this section we examined some of these functional groups in terms of three general parts of the brain: (1) the spinal cord, (2) the brainstem and (3) the forebrain. We looked at the nervous system comparatively from species to species and also in various stages of development and considered functions of various parts of the brain. The autonomic nervous system, comprising the sympathetic division and the parasympathetic division, is a prime controller of our basic life functions. Without it the autonomic bodily machinery of which we are generally unaware, would cease to operate.

The somatic nervous system and the central nervous system are responsible for the expression of our daily behavior, and unlike the autonomic nervous system, are under our voluntary control. We saw that nerve cells are of three kinds: (1) sensory neurons, (2) motor neurons and (3) interneurons. Motor and sensory pathways cross from one side of the body to the other side of the brain. The level of sophistication of information-processing increases in the structures higher up into the brain, culminating in the neocortex, which is highly developed in the human brain where it is much larger than in that of most other species. The neocortical surface is organized into a receptortopic pattern. Each of the four neocortical lobes has special jobs.

≡ *Input to Brain*

Much of what we are and do is the result of our interactions with the environment. A major influence on our reaction to the world is the way in which we perceive it. We only know the world via our nervous system. If our nerves convey misinformation, we perceive a distorted picture of the world as reality. Thus, the way in which our nervous system responds to the environment, the way in which it codes sensory information, and the kind of "central processing" the brain does, forms our conception of the world—we have no other.

Vision

Of the sensory systems to be considered here—vision, hearing, touch and the so-called chemical senses—we know the most about the visual system. This is so because of the obvious importance of vision to humans and because it is more readily studied than the other senses. The stimuli to which the human eye responds are within a limited segment of the electromagnetic spectrum—namely, the radiation of wavelengths from about 380 to 760 nanometers (a nanometer is 10^{-9} meter). (The total range of wavelengths in the electromagnetic spectrum is from 0.00005 nanometers to several miles!) This narrow segment of the spectrum contains all the colors seen by the human eye (some animals can see in the infrared and ultraviolet). The eye is not equally sensitive to all colors, being most sensitive to yellow-green as shown in Figure 23.

The human eye is an exquisite, complex sphere, actually a miniature brain in itself. Light enters the eye through the *cornea,* a transparent tissue that performs most of the bending of light necessary to form an image on the *retina* (the light-sensitive portion of the eye). The *lens,* a remarkably elastic, transparent structure, whose construction is similar to that of an onion, does the final focusing.

Colors	Wavelength (nanometers)	Sensitivity of the human eye

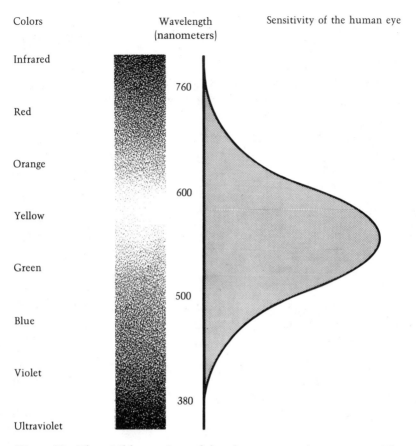

Infrared

760

Red

Orange

600

Yellow

Green

500

Blue

Violet

380

Ultraviolet

Figure 23 The visible portion of the electromagnetic spectrum. The graph shows the relative sensitivity of the human eye to color. (We are most sensitive to yellow-green.)

The image formed on the retina is "upside down and backwards" as a result of passing through the lens. The lens permits precise focusing by changing its shape from spheroid (for close viewing, such as when reading this book) to more flattened (when at rest or focusing on a distant scene). Tiny muscles attached to the edge of the lens are responsible for this ability. Like all muscles, they can become fatigued from prolonged overuse, causing pain or eyestrain. With advancing age the lens loses some of its inherent elastic ability and is incapable of changing its shape sufficiently to bring near objects into correct focus.

Try bringing this page closer and closer to your eyes. Have someone measure the distance from your eye to the page when it is as close as it can be with the words in sharp focus. Then find a person much older or much younger than you are and have him or her repeat the experiment. Compare the measured distances.

The cells of the retina act as transducers. A transducer changes one form of energy into another. A stereo cartridge transduces motion (from the wiggling grooves) into electricity. The nervous system employs a variety of transducers in its response to external forms of energy.

The transduction of light energy into neural activity is carried out by specialized structures (known as receptors) in the retina. In the eye there are two varieties of receptors: *rods* and *cones*. As a result of light stimulation, the receptors generate minute electrical potentials that, if sufficiently large, give rise to an action potential in the sensory neuron, which, in turn, activates the brain. The rods and cones are differentially sensitive. Rods are extremely sensitive to dim light and convey no sense of color, but rather, only black and white sensations. Most of us rarely use pure rod vision since in our cities even the nights are too "bright"; a sufficiently dark location would be in the country under a full moon. The receptors you are using at this moment, unless you have rather unusual study habits, are cones. These receptors are more sensitive at greater intensities of illumination and are responsible for color and detailed vision.

Rods and cones are unequally represented over the retina (Figure 24). A small area directly on the visual axis (the *fovea*) contains only tightly packed cones. Hold your arm straight out and look directly at your thumbnail. The image of your thumbnail is now projected onto, and covers, the fovea. The number of cones falls off rapidly, moving along the retina away from the fovea. Rods are thus excluded from the fovea, but appear in large numbers immediately adjacent to it. This concentration of rods just off the visual axis explains the observation that a very dim star

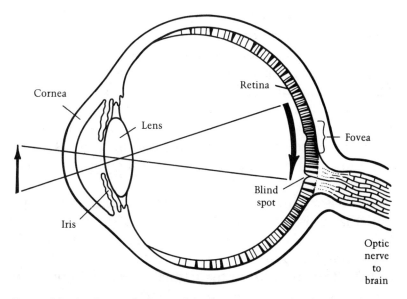

Figure 24 An internal view of the human eye. The fovea is the region of best-detailed vision. The fovea has no rods but has the greatest density of cones. The rods are most dense about 20 degrees away from the fovea. Note that the lens of the eye inverts the image on the retina.

"cannot be seen" by looking directly at it—the observer must look slightly to the side. The faint light from the star does not activate the cones but rather, the more sensitive rods.

Both rods and cones contain chemicals that have the unusual property of changing their molecular arrangement upon exposure to light; these are termed *photochemicals*. If you had a test tube full of the rod photochemical and watched it as it was brought out of darkness into light, you would see a change from deep purple to a lighter shade, as if it were being "bleached." This in fact is what is happening, with light doing the molecular bleaching. If we allowed light to bleach as much of the photochemical as possible (until it stopped becoming paler) and then placed it back into the dark, time and the necessary enzymes would be needed for it to "unbleach" or to re-form the original photochemical. Thirty minutes of darkness are needed to reconstitute the test-tube photochemical. This is the same length of time required for a human to establish maximal sensitivity to dim light. There are three varieties of cones, each with its own photochemical: one each for red, green and blue. Whereas light of almost any wavelength bleaches the rod photochemical, the green cone is maximally bleached by green light and is much less sensitive to other colors. Our awareness of the visual world is determined, in part, by the actions of the photochemicals as they influence the nervous system.

It is a general rule for all sensory (and motor) systems that most of the information from the right side of the body travels to the left hemisphere of the brain, and vice versa. This generality holds true for the visual system. Visual information from the left half of the field of vision is processed in the right hemisphere, and that from the right visual field is processed in the left hemisphere (see Figure 25).

When we look at something, its image is projected onto the retina upside down and backwards; the image nonetheless is an accurate representation of the visual world. The projected image activates the rods and cones, and, in turn, the retinal neurons that extend into the brain. This spatial representation of the visual world on the retina is preserved in the neocortex. The fovea has a very large neocortical area—no doubt the reason we are capable of seeing so much detail from objects in the line of sight.

Color vision Since various combinations of light of the three primary colors (red, green and blue) will produce any color in the visible spectrum, it is not too surprising that three kinds of cones have been discovered, each being most sensitive to a particular wavelength. Other colors can be seen because information arising from the three cone types is combined and compared. Some individuals are born color-blind. These people lack one or more of the cone types in their retina and see colors differently as a result.

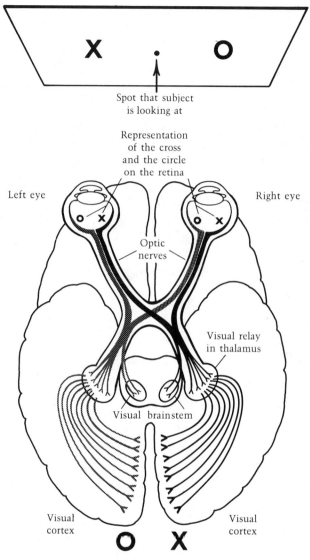

Phantom view of brain from top

Figure 25 The human visual pathway. Images from the right half of the visual field are focused on the left side of each retina. The neural information from these two left sides travels to the left hemisphere of the brain via a relay in the thalamus. Similarly, the left half of the visual field is processed in the right cerebral cortex. The retina also sends axons into the visual area of the brainstem. (Adapted from "The Neurophysiology of Binocular Vision" by J. D. Pettigrew. Copyright 1972 by Scientific American, Inc. All rights reserved.)

Adaptation We are all aware that the familiar, the commonplace, doesn't receive much attention—our interest is attracted to the new, the changing, the fashionable. The retina, too, seems to be afflicted with the "Madison Avenue syndrome" in that a constantly moving projection of the world shifts across it because of small, imperceptible movements of the eye. Your eyes are making such movements right now, but you are unaware of it. If these movements were to stop, as in the experiment illustrated in Figure 26, you would not be able to read these words, or in fact see much of anything. This points up a rather important characteristic of most receptors—rapid *adaptation*. By this is meant the tendency to cease responding to an unchanging stimulus.

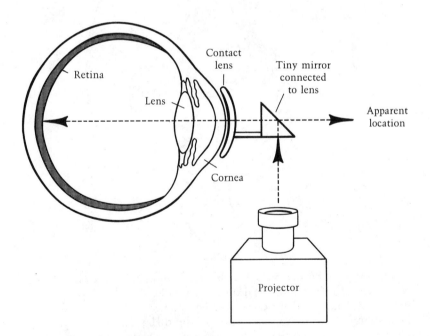

Figure 26 Stabilized image experiment. The small, rapid movements of the eye are compensated for by a mirror mounted on a contact lens. This result is greatly impaired vision—the image waxes and wanes and often simply disappears.

That receptors have this property is fortunate for those of us who must wash sweaty gym socks, change diapers, eat someone's terrible cooking, wear clothes or sit down. The irritation of clothes on your skin or the pressure of the chair upon your buttocks might be unbearable save for rapid receptor adaptation. Indeed it is not likely that you are at this moment aware of the pressure of the clothes on your back; if, however, you move, thus providing the appropriate stimulus to the receptor—a changing sensory pattern—you may become aware of it. Aside from its usefulness in unpleasant situations, adaptation, in general, attunes the nervous system to new or changing stimuli while not burdening the brain with unchanging stimuli. A similar phenomenon, habituation, was discussed earlier. To distinguish the two forms of response decrement, remember that adaptation is a property of the sensory receptor becoming insensitive, whereas habituation is a process occurring not at the sensory receptor, but within the central nervous system.

Visual cortex We know something of the way in which the visual system works from experiments in which recordings were made of the electrical activity of individual neurons in the visual neocortex of cats, whose visual system is much like our own. These experiments by David Hubel and Torsen Weisel, who shared the 1981 Nobel Prize for their work, showed that single neurons in the cortex respond to very specific kinds of stimuli: moving lines, rectangles or wedges of light projected on a screen (Figure 27). The visual neocortex is organized into regions—in some areas the neurons respond to simple stimuli (lines) and in others to more complex stimuli (moving shapes). The same kinds of responses were seen in newborn kittens who had no visual experience prior to the experiment. This rules out the possibility that the neurons developed these response patterns to specific stimuli as a result of experience. The environment, however, can change such inborn response patterns. Young cats were

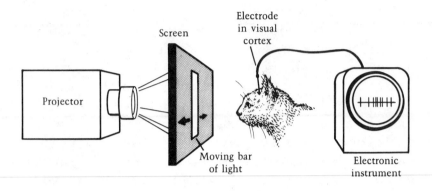

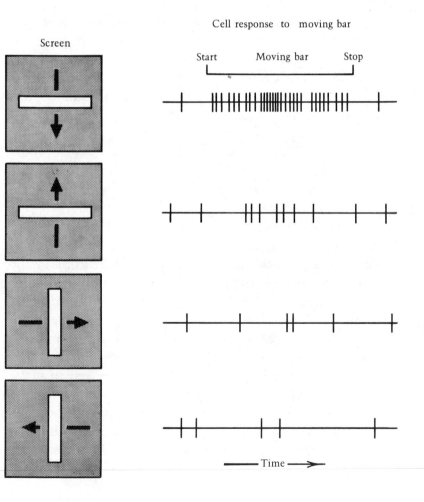

Figure 27 Visual form reception by single neurons in the visual area of the neocortex. A small electrode inserted in the visual cortex of an anesthetized cat picks up action potentials of single neurons activated by stimuli presented to the eye. The electronic instrument, which is similar to a television set, shows firing of single neurons. The lower part of the illustration shows the response of a complex-stimuli cell to a moving bar of light. This particular cell responds most strongly to a horizontal bar moving in a downward direction.

reared in a room containing only horizontal bars. Visual neocortex neurons were later examined for responses to horizontal and vertical bars. There were few "vertical neurons" and many "horizontal neurons," implying that the nervous system was functionally changed by an unusual environment. As you might expect, the kittens' behavior reflected this alteration in the nervous system. For example, the kittens were functionally blind to a stick held vertically, yet would bat at it in a normal fashion when held horizontally.

The importance of these discoveries is that we see the world as we do because our visual system is wired in a certain way. This wiring of the brain seems complete at birth as shown in the kitten study. It now appears likely that our visual perception of the world is in large part genetically determined. Nevertheless, the environment can act upon, and modify, the brain. It thus appears that neurons of the visual portion of the brain are genetically prewired but subject to modification by the environment.

Hearing

Like vision, hearing is a sensory system receiving information from distant sources. This is in contrast to touch or taste, wherein direct stimulation of the body surface or interior is conveyed to the brain. Hearing, although not as debilitating as vision when absent in humans, conveys to our brain a great deal of information about the external world.

The stimuli that we hear are actually compressions and rarefactions of air molecules, commonly termed sound waves. Figure 28 depicts sound waves created by the forward motion (compression) and backward motion (rarefaction) of the cone of a loudspeaker. Sound waves travel at about 1,000 feet per second and are characterized by having a frequency (or pitch) and intensity (or loud-

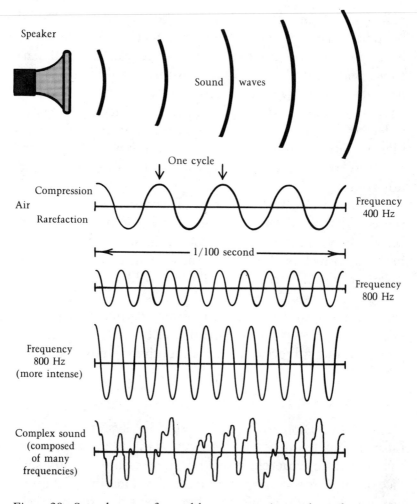

Figure 28 Sound waves formed by compression and rarefaction of the molecules of the air. Shown in the lower part are sound waves varying in frequency and intensity.

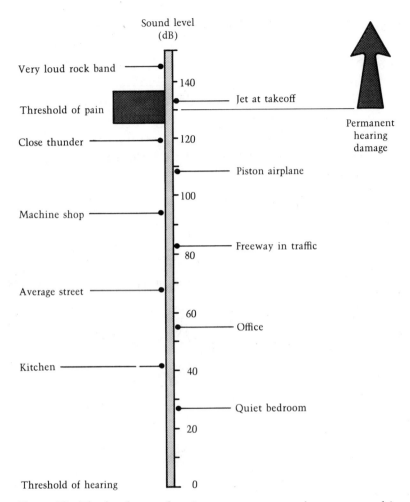

Figure 29 The loudness of various common sounds as measured in decibels.

ness). Frequency is specified in cycles (from compression to rarefaction) per second (you will see this abbreviated Hz). A young human can hear frequencies from 20 to 20,000 Hz. Intensity is rated on a decibel (dB) scale from 0 (the threshold of hearing) to 160 (the level of immediate and permanent damage to the human ear). Figure 29 shows the loudness of common sounds as measured in decibels. With advancing age, high-frequency hearing declines. More generalized hearing damage occurs as a result of exposure to very loud sounds. The longer the exposure, the more the damage. Musicians in rock bands, for example, are in danger of hearing impairments unless they take protective measures.

The ear is conveniently divided into three components: external, middle and inner (Figure 30). The external ear consists of the *pinna,* an elaborately formed cartilaginous appendage that serves little function in humans, but

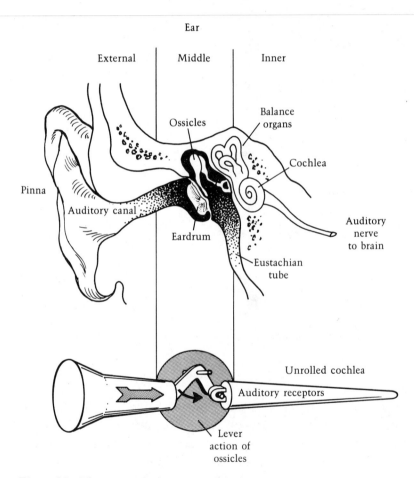

Figure 30   The general structure of the ear. The actual receptor mechanism is in the coiled cochlea. The lower part of the illustration shows a schematic diagram of the ear. The ossicles of the middle ear transmit vibrations from the eardrum into the cochlea.

is quite important in animals more attuned to auditory stimuli. Many animals can move the pinna to a remarkable degree (observe a domestic cat or a German shepherd). In these animals the pinna acts as a "funnel" for sound waves entering the *auditory canal*. The eardrum marks the boundary between the external and middle ear. It is a taut membrane that vibrates at the frequency of the arriving sound waves. These minute vibrations (the smallest are less than one-tenth the diameter of the hydrogen atom) are transmitted to the *cochlea* of the inner ear via the body *ossicles* of the middle ear. The ossicles, three in number, act as a complicated lever, increasing the force of the vibrations. The ossicle lever is necessary because the inner ear is filled with fluid, and more force is required to drive the vibrations through the fluid.

The neural receptors for the ear are cells bearing sensory hairs at their apexes. These hair cells are located on the *basilar membrane* in the spiral-like cochlea of the inner ear. When vibrations are forced through the fluid of the cochlea by the ossicles, the basilar membrane vibrates, activating the hair cells against the *tectorial membrane* (Figure 31). Different frequencies are represented at different positions on the basilar membrane. From the cochlea, the impulses generated by these stimuli travel via the auditory nerve into the brainstem and are relayed to many structures. The auditory pathways terminate in the temporal lobes of the cortex.

The human ear is most sensitive to only a part of the total range of sound waves—namely, the part from 1,000 to 4,000 Hz (the range of the human voice and most musical instruments). Other animals have different ranges of greatest sensitivity, coinciding with their ranges of vocalization. Small animals, such as mice, that generally emit high-frequency sounds tend to have the greatest sensitivity for high frequencies. Larger animals that tend to bellow and roar are most sensitive to low frequencies. Each species of animal has a total range of hearing that is somewhat greater than its range of greatest sensitivity. These total

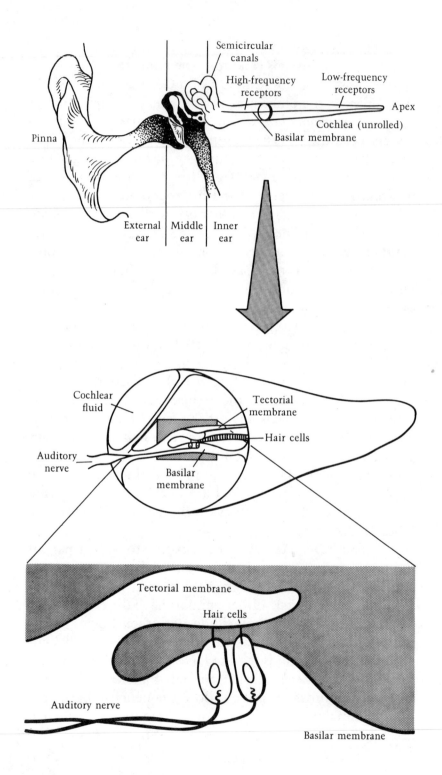

Figure 31 A diagram of the ear showing the cochlea "unrolled."
The neural receptors are located on the basilar membrane. High
frequencies are received near the pinna end of the basilar
membrane. Low frequencies are received near the apex. The
exploded view of the cochlea shows the tectorial membrane resting
on the basilar membrane of the cochlea. The actual sound
transduction takes place via hair cells embedded in the basilar
membrane, which are activated by being pressed against the
tectorial membrane sending neural impulses out the auditory nerve
to the brain.

ranges also differ, of course, from species to species, in the
directions that would be expected from consideration of
differences in greatest sensitivity.

A pure tone (that is, one of single frequency) does
not activate the basilar membrane and the tectorial membrane along the entire length of the cochlea, but rather,
only a limited area of these membranes begins to vibrate.
The locations at which various frequencies cause the membranes to vibrate can be mapped; these are also, of course,
the locations of the receptors (the hair cells) that generate
the corresponding neural impulses. It has been found that
receptors for high frequencies are located near the ossicles
and those for low frequencies at the far end of the membranes (clearly depicted in Figure 31 with the cochlea "unrolled"). Thus, hair cells are selectively activated by particular frequencies. Frequencies lower than about 1,000
Hz, however, simultaneously stimulate all hair cells of the
human cochlea. In these two ways, selective activation for
higher frequencies and simultaneous activation for lower
frequencies, the hair cells are able to convey precise information about frequencies to the brain. Most sounds are
not pure tones but composites of many frequencies; the
brain processes with apparent ease the complicated information that results.

The coding of stimulus intensity is the same for all
senses: the brain deciphers intensity information from (1)
the number of neurons that are active, (2) the rapidity with
which they fire and (3) the activity of special neurons that

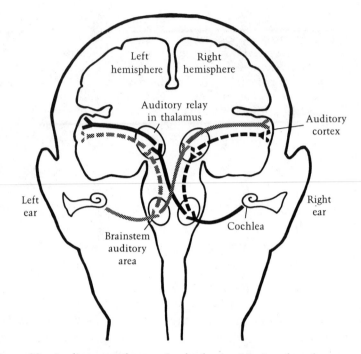

Figure 32 Auditory pathways in the brain. Notice that these
pathways are not all crossed (see dashed lines), but the most
powerful auditory input goes to the opposite hemisphere, that is,
right ear to left hemisphere. (Adapted from "The Asymmetry of
the Human Brain" by D. Kimura. Copyright 1973 by Scientific
American, Inc. All rights reserved.)

have a "high threshold," that is, they fire only when the
stimulus is intense. Auditory pathways are shown in Figure 32; the most powerful input is from the ear on one side
of the head to the hemisphere on the opposite side.

On the neocortical region specialized for processing
auditory information and located on the temporal lobe,
the cochlea is spatially represented several times in strips,
corresponding to high-to-low frequencies. Thus, the neocortex duplicates a representation of the auditory world
found in the cochlea. This is a general feature of the senses.
You will recall that a representation of the visual world
received by the retina is passed on to the visual region of
the neocortex.

The ear is exquisitely sensitive. At the threshold of hearing, the ear can detect energy levels equivalent to the energy represented by the light from a candle eight miles away. In fact, if the ear were any more sensitive than it is, we would be continuously assailed by our own bodily noises—blood pouring through veins and arteries, heart pumping, breath rushing in and out—and by the random bombardment of air molecules against the eardrums. It is possible in a totally soundproof and echo-free room for a person (just barely) to hear these sounds. Normally background noise masks them.

Touch

If a forefinger is gently touched to your arm, you interpret this as "touch." You also can describe the temperature and texture of the finger. If the forefinger is pressed into your arm, you may report feeling "pressure." If the pressure is increased further at some point, you might cry out in pain. Touch comprises these varied but related sensations. These, as opposed to vision and hearing, do not inform you of distant events but rather, of objects directly touching the body surface. In addition to the touch system is a receptor network that tells the brain of the position of the limbs in space and the degree of muscular tension in each muscle. This latter receptor network serving the kinesthetic sense will be discussed in detail later.

For many years it was thought that the varied sensations of touch—temperature, texture, pressure and pain—were each detected by specialized receptors of the skin. Such specialized receptors can be identified with the microscope. However, it was shown that a person can experience touch, temperature and pain from the cornea of the eye—an area that has no specialized receptors but only nonspecialized nerve endings. Specialized receptors in the skin may communicate particular sensations, but they are not necessary for the brain's recognition of the particular sensations, as the cornea experiments show. The body surface is not equally sensitive in all parts to touch, hands and lips being the most sensitive and best equipped to detect small differences in objects; the back and thighs are poorly equipped to detect differences. This is so because the hands and lips have many receptors and the back and thighs have few.

Somatic cortex We have seen that the visual and auditory receptor systems (retina and cochlea) are "laid out" on the surface of the brain. And, as already described in the introductory discussion of the neocortex, the same holds true for the *somatic sensory system* (the touch system). As receptors for touch are located all over the surface of the body, it is not too surprising that the body surface is represented on the surface of the neocortex. The body layout on the brain is distorted because the brain allocates cortical space not in terms of anatomical size, but in terms of receptor density. As Figure 20 shows, neocortical areas for human hands and lips are exaggerated in comparison to the physical proportions of these parts, but this "exaggeration" represents their biological importance. Thus, such animals as rodents that explore the world largely by sniffing and poking their whisker-rich noses into things have relatively enormous neocortical areas for the nose. Similarly, the somatic sensory cortex of tree-living monkeys is taken up largely by areas for fore- and hind-limb digits, which are very important in an arboreal way of life.

If in an experiment, the left-hand area of a human somatic sensory cortex were electrically stimulated, the person serving as the experimental subject would report feeling "something" in the right hand—an ill-defined sensation far removed from the precise sensory information we obtain by merely brushing our fingertips rapidly across an object. Soon, it is hoped, scientists may be able to tell us more about the operation of the touch system.

Kinesthetic Sense

The *kinesthetic sense* is concerned with the orientation and location of the different parts of the body, especially the limbs. The brain must keep track of the relative position of the parts while the body is engaging in activity. The brain must know the position of the limbs before they can be moved to a new position; it must also know to maintain balance when there is no limb movement. The receptors for the kinesthetic sense are located in the joints, the tendons and the muscles. We are often consciously unaware of the kinesthetic sense, although we use it continually in our daily activities. The same is true of the *vestibular sense,* the organs near the ear that allow us to maintain balance.

Chemical Senses

The *chemical senses* are smell and taste. The stimuli to which they respond are molecules suspended in either air or liquid. Relatively little is known about the chemical senses, compared to the others, probably because incapacitating damage to these senses is rare, thus reducing a prime motivation for study. Humans, as a species, are not noted for a well-developed sense of smell. Most mammals far surpass our olfactory abilities. In the wild, smell of predator or prey may be an animal's first cue and one that comes from quite a distance, alerting it long before vision or hearing are effective. In many species, smell is critical for behaviors related to mating, eating, species identification, "family group" identification and territorial marking.

Taste—at least for the human species—is at once a critical and a relatively unimportant sense. It is critical in the sense that it exerts some control over what a person eats. Through the sense of taste, people divide foods into categories as to whether or not the food is liked. Taste thus determines our diet to some extent. And, as someone has noted, "you are what you eat." This is quite literally true!

Yet taste is relatively unimportant in that much of what we think is taste is actually smell. The classic demonstration is to blindfold someone, plug the subject's nose, present an onion and a potato to eat, and ask if the subject can taste the difference. The reply will be "no" and should be enough to convince even the skeptic. Another large component of "taste" is the activation of pressure receptors in the mouth (the texture of food is an important determinant of its palatability), and, with foods that are too hot or spicy, the activation of pain receptors.

The olfactory receptors are so located in the upper regions of the nasal cavity that during normal breathing, little air reaches them (Figure 33). Sniffing changes nasal airflow and bathes the receptors with the molecules that are in the air. The neurons leading from these receptors go to an extension of the brain known as the *olfactory bulb*. The means by which the receptors and olfactory bulb respond to and code olfactory information remains a mys-

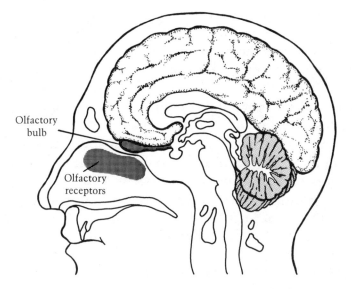

Figure 33 The olfactory brain. The olfactory receptors are located in the upper portion of the nasal cavity and have neural connections to the olfactory bulb, which lies below the frontal lobes of the brain.

tery. This is not to say that there are no ideas or theories about the workings of the olfactory sense; on the contrary, there are a great many theories. The number of theories explaining a particular phenomenon may in fact be directly related to the amount of ignorance regarding the phenomenon! In olfaction, the predominant theory asserts that the shape of molecules—that is, their stereochemistry—is important in olfactory sensations.

The molecules that we smell are suspended in air. The molecules that we "taste" are suspended in liquid, generally water or saliva. Taste receptors are located primarily on the tongue in specialized structures termed *taste buds*. Although we can identify a great number of dissolved substances as each having a unique taste, these can all be expressed as various combinations of four basic tastes: sweet, sour, salty and bitter.

The sense of taste offers a good example of a principle of brain functioning—adaptation. If we eat mouthful after mouthful of a single food, its taste soon becomes less "strong" or "noticeable." This lessening response is receptor adaptation, a decrease in receptor output during long exposure to a stimulus. The corollary is that the nervous system responds best to change. Coffee tasters have known this for centuries and rinse their mouth with water between tastes in order not only to remove any remainder of the previous sip of coffee but also to maintain the taste receptors in their most sensitive, nonadapted state.

☰ Summary

☰ *In this section we have examined the senses by which we know the external world. We have seen that the eye is an exquisite little brain in itself, containing two kinds of photoreceptors: rods and cones. These receptors contain photochemicals that translate light energy into neural impulses. The visual cortex is so organized—apparently from birth—that it can respond to rather complex visual stimuli without having any prior experience with these stimuli. The ear, too, is a very complex and sensitive structure. The receptors for hearing, found in the co-chlea, are hair cells that convert vibrations into neural impulses. From the cochlea, information travels to the auditory cortex and is "displayed" upon the neocortical surface.*

Other sensory systems operate under the same basic rules as vision and hearing. The touch system is projected onto the somatic cortex in a receptortopic way. Relative areas allotted in the map of the body surface on the neocortex express the sensitivity of the various body parts rather than their physical size. The kinesthetic sense and the chemical senses also contribute information about the external world.

Brain Processing

Brain scientists currently know a good deal about sensory systems in the brain and as we shall see, about motor systems connecting brain to muscle. About what lies in between, we know considerably less. Yet, the vast bulk of the human brain, estimated at over 80% of brain tissue, is concerned with the processing of information received from sensory systems prior to delivery to motor systems. These regions of the brain appear to be devoted to information processing. In Figure 22, for example, the stippled areas indicate those regions of the brain that are concerned primarily with information processing. As you can see, the amount of neocortical brain matter devoted to processing increases dramatically from rat to human.

What sorts of neuronal happenings occur in these processing regions? The neuronal activities underlying thought, language, dreaming and the like probably occur in these regions. As stated earlier, we know that damage to regions of the human neocortex will result in problems in perception and language. But reaching a more detailed level of neuronal operations requires something more sophisticated than looking at what happens to someone with a damaged brain. How are the neurons behaving in these regions of the brain that process input signals into language?

We do not know the answer to this question. What we do know is that the brain appears to analyze incoming information in a hierarchical manner. That is to say, a meaningful pattern is built up gradually from the basic elements supplied by brain input systems. Let's take a visual example. We saw earlier that there are cells in the cortex that respond preferentially to the orientation of a line as viewed on a screen. Some cells respond best to horizontal lines, some to vertical lines, others to lines of intermediate orientations. One can also find cells in the brain that respond best to angles. A cell responding to a right angle, for instance, could well be receiving synaptic input from two different cells, one of which responds best to a horizontal line, the other which responds best to a vertical line. Given the proper orientation, a horizontal and a vertical line will make a right angle. It is conceivable that several such cells could work together to encode the essence of a square or a rectangle or any geometric figure. The image of a book, for example, can be thought of as a series of lines and angles all of which could be built up from the simple line and edge detectors discussed in the previous sections (Figure 34).

The evidence for such complex cells is difficult to come by. What examples there are, however, are quite illuminating. One brain scientist reported locating a neuron in a processing region of the brain which frustrated his every attempt to determine what its optimal visual stimulus was. Finally, in exasperation, he threw up his hands in dismay while happening to be in the animal's visual field. At that moment, the cell fired a burst of action potentials. Intrigued, Dr. Charlie Gross proceeded to discover that the optimal stimulus for this particular cell was a cardboard silhouette of the monkey's hand! In another experiment, recording the activity of single neurons from processing areas of the neocortex, Dr. Richard Thompson discovered that a small percentage of the cells he encountered (about 1%) seemed to respond to the concept of number. That is, some cells would fire a burst of action

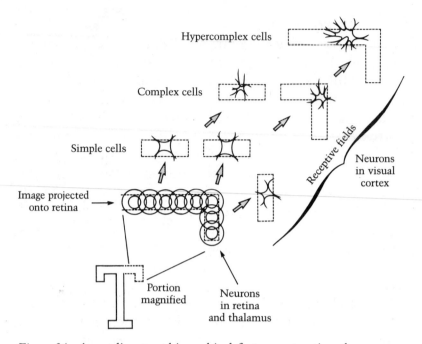

Figure 34 According to a hierarchical feature extraction theory, neurons in the visual system respond to elementary aspects of the visual image. Each succeeding hierarchy receives information from more elementary feature extraction cells. In such a theoretical model, all of the neurons are required to work together to achieve a visual sensation/perception.

potentials on the fifth stimulus presentation, other cells fired to the seventh or ninth stimulus presentation (flashes of lights or tone bursts), regardless of the rate at which those stimuli were delivered. The conclusion is that those cells were responding to the abstract concept of number rather than to any other feature of the stimulus. A difficulty with both of the examples just cited is, of course, that we can never present all of the possible stimulus combinations to a given cell and can thus never be sure that we have hit upon the optimal stimulus.

Dr. Vernon Mountcastle and others have studied a processing region of the neocortex whose cells respond only when an animal is watching an object that is important to it. The cell will fire only when the animal directs its visual attention to a particular stimulus. Presumably, these cells are involved in some aspect of the animal's paying attention to a stimulus that is meaningful. Not all processing activity occurs in the neocortex by any means. However, in the human, the amount of neocortical material far exceeds the bulk of other neural structures and represents the major processing area in the brain. Only whales and dolphins possess nearly comparable brains.

☰ *Output from Brain*

☰ The most direct agents in the expression of behavior are the muscles of the skeleton. Skeletal muscles of themselves cannot cause movement—they are under the direction of the nervous system. A command comes from the central nervous system via motor neurons in the spinal cord. An action potential from a spinal motor neuron releases transmitter chemical onto the muscle, which then contracts (see pages 36–44). Some of our movements are reflexive and do not require participation of the brain, but all of our voluntary behaviors originate in the brain. The messages are routed out of the brain by the pathways of two output systems, which end in the spinal cord—the pyramidal system and extrapyramidal system.

Far more is understood about the simpler of the two systems, the *pyramidal system*. It has its origin in the motor area of the frontal neocortex where, just as we have described for the somatic cortex, various areas represent different parts of the body. The neocortical representation of the body, the homunculus for the motor system, is roughly that of a prone body stretched along the frontal lobe at the border of the parietal lobe. A homunculus on the right hemisphere represents the left side of the body and one on the left hemisphere represents the right side. Pyramidal-system neurons in the motor cortex have long axons that extend through the brain and deep into the spinal cord. In humans these axons are as long as 3 feet, and in large whales as long as 30 feet! It is amazing that such cells can even exist. Remember, the nerve cell's machinery, which must look after a lengthy axon, is contained within the cell body.

The *extrapyramidal system* is much more complex than the pyramidal system, and less is known about it. Basically, it consists of many neurons originating deep within the brain in regions under the cortex and having axons that extend into the spinal cord where they interact with the pyramidal axons to produce movement. The pyramidal and extrapyramidal output systems (which we may refer to collectively as the motor system) make extensive use of feedback, a phenomenon familiar to the engineer and encountered in the discussion of biofeedback in a previous section. Biofeedback as employed in medicine is purely informational, that is, the signal itself does not effect any change; it only provides otherwise unavailable information about the activity of organs. In contrast, a device may actually be controlled by means of the feeding back into it of the results of its operation. In the body this process is known as *homeostasis*—the maintenance of relatively constant conditions within the body. Virtually every home has an example of a feedback device within the heating system of the house—the thermostat. You set the thermostat to warm the house to a particular temperature (termed the *set point* in biological systems). The furnace then proceeds to heat the house. When the thermostat detects that the temperature which you designated (the set point) has been reached, it turns the furnace off until the temperature falls and then the process repeats itself. The motor system uses feedback to compare the actual positions of limbs with the desired positions to which they are to be moved. The amount and pattern of contraction of the muscles in the limb are determined by continual comparisons of this sort.

The motor system is in full operation even when a person is standing still. The muscles and tendons have receptors that signal the motor system about their state of contraction; the balance receptors in the head signal the motor system about the body's balance and about how weight must be shifted in order to maintain it; receptors of the eyes, the pressure receptors on the bottom of the feet and receptors that sense the pull of gravity on the limbs all feed signals back to the motor system that assist in the maintenance of upright posture (Figure 35). When you

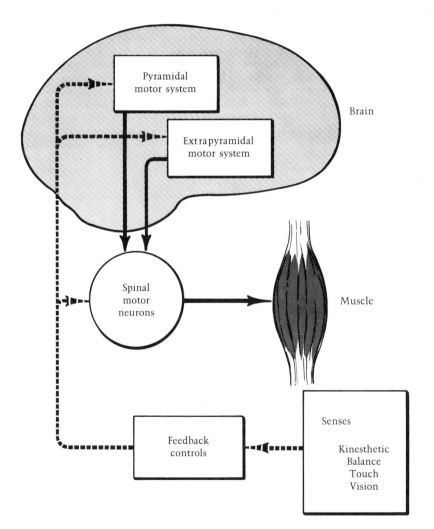

Figure 35 A schematic diagram of the motor systems of the brain connected to the spinal motor neurons and thus to muscle. The motor system of the brain is characterized by extensive use of feedback controls to regulate movements of the organism.

undertake a voluntary movement, all of these kinds of receptors participate as do the brain centers that evaluate the signals in comparison with the desired movement. And miraculously enough, all of this takes place without your giving it much attention.

When you reach for a glass of water, you do not consciously think about moving forward 4 inches and to the side 3 inches and rotating your wrist 47 degrees and extending your fingers and grasping with enough force to hold the glass firmly without breaking it, and so forth. No—you simply "will it" and it is done! It is almost as if there were a beautifully designed and executed choreography being coordinated expertly by a fine director. The brain sciences cannot, as of yet, explain how these movements are programmed and set into motion by the brain. And yet, these are simple movements. Consider the movements made by the accomplished pianist, the rapid typist, the person delivering a speech, the hurdle jumper or the tennis player.

Electrical stimulation of the human brain has provided insight into the operation of the motor cortex. Pioneering studies showed that stimulation produced movements in a body part corresponding to the portion of the homunculus stimulated. The movements were not jerky twitches; rather, they were integrated and directed movements often entailing whole sets of muscles acting in concert. The subjects felt no pain and were often surprised and mildly annoyed at the behavior of, say, one of their arms, resulting from stimulation. They felt as if the arm were "acting by itself." It was as if they were casual observers of someone else's arm. Indeed, the voluntary control of a subject had no part in the movement; it was produced by the electrical current.

——— Summary
———
——— *Earlier in this book we examined the muscles and how they contract. We know that muscles do not contract on their own, but rather, require impulses from the nervous system to set*

them into activity. In this section we have seen how the brain organizes its output to the muscles. There are two output systems, the pyramidal and extrapyramidal systems. The origin of these systems is primarily the motor cortex of the frontal lobe and areas underlying the neocortex. The map of the motor cortex is a homunculus very similar to the somatosensory homunculus. Here, too, the figure is distorted, expressing the relative precision of movement possible in the various body parts. The motor system of the brain makes extensive use of feedback controls to keep the body operating in a normal and coordinated manner.

Brain Motivational Systems

Why do we eat? Drink? Aspire? Mate? The answers to these questions constitute an area of research concerned with the motivation or causes of behavior. Motivation is not something we can weigh or measure. We see an animal eating and we infer that it is eating because it is hungry. Although such inferences may serve us well for simple behaviors exhibited by "simple" creatures, they may totally fail us when we are observing humans. Consider watching a friend eat lunch. We may assume she is eating lunch because she is hungry. However, we may discover that she is having lunch only because she relishes peanut-butter sandwiches. She actually was not hungry at all.

A man sitting at her table is not eating. Do we infer that he is not hungry? We had better not. He may have forgotten to bring his lunch or his lunch money, or perhaps he is on a strict diet and is actually quite hungry. The point is that it is unreliable to infer human motives solely from observed behavior. To infer from observed behavior what motivates a person who is going to school, climbing a mountain or raising a child is tantamount to folly.

Brain scientists are actively trying to provide some measurable underpinning to the quest for the causes of behavior. The search is in the initial phases. It would not be wise to attempt to understand an automobile engine without first understanding levers, gears and cams. Similarly, workers in the neurosciences are trying to understand the causes of simple behaviors in animals rather than complex behaviors in humans.

Every animal has needs that must be fulfilled by the environment. These include food, water, air and a viable range of temperatures. These needs are based on the requirements of tissues and must be met, at least minimally, or the animal will die. The meeting of these requirements ensures (barring accidents) the survival of the individual organism.

Survival of the species depends upon successful reproductive behavior, which is usually accompanied by innate or learned social behaviors. One of the functions of social behaviors is to place male and female in proximity, a requisite for mating. Social behaviors can also provide group cohesiveness and protection from danger. All these functions may be necessary for successful mating and rearing of young.

We know a great deal about the brain mechanisms resulting in simple behaviors such as eating, drinking and mating among animals. It is assumed that in time the brain mechanisms underlying more complex behaviors will also be understood. Let us turn to a simple behavior—eating. A basic requirement of an animal is to ingest substances that will meet its tissues' need for an energy source. The question becomes one of how the brain detects the body's need for food and how it directs a coordinated series of behaviors that culminate in the ingestion of food.

Eating

It was once thought that people eat to relieve "hunger pangs," the sensations associated with the contractions of an empty stomach. The logical experiment was to place a balloon in the stomach, inflate it, record changes in air pressure within the balloon as indications of contractions, and compare these "hunger pangs" with the subject's report of being hungry. The initial experiments seemed to disprove the hypothesis that stomach contractions were associated with hunger. What scientists found was that the balloon showed the stomach to be continuously contracting! Later experiments using a somewhat different balloon correctly reported that stomach contractions were associated with feelings of hunger. The initial misleading experiment demonstrates a problem often encountered by scientists—that a measuring device may interfere with what is being measured. In the initial experiments the mere presence of the balloon in the stomach triggered reflex contractions. Such reflex contractions normally follow the arrival of food in the stomach. The problem was resolved by redesigning the balloon to get around the difficulty.

The interference from measuring devices is a serious problem that is often difficult to assess—especially in a human social setting. Another example of such interference comes from an experiment performed in a large industrial plant. In an effort to identify factors that would increase production, the management set up one production line in a special area where they played music, tried various decorating schemes and so forth. The result of this effort was that production increased remarkably, regardless of what was done. In fact, if nothing was changed from the normal work area, production in the special line was greater anyway! The problem was that the employees knew they were being evaluated while they were working in the special line, and this seems to have motivated them to produce more. Here, too, the measuring device, in the form of the experimental production line, interfered with what the experimenters wished to measure.

To return to our discussion of eating, most of us prefer to eat a hot hamburger rather than a cold one because it tastes better. Thus, it comes as no surprise that taste is a major factor controlling eating. An animal will consistently choose a "good-tasting" diet over a "bad-tasting" one when both contain equal food value. Indeed, one of the principal objections to the projected use of plankton farmed from the oceans (which is quite nutritious) is that it does not have a pleasing flavor. Although taste exerts some control over eating, there are other factors operating as well. A rat, for instance, will learn to reject a "good-tasting" food if it subsequently makes him sick. It will also learn to prefer a "bad-tasting" food with nutritive value to a "good-tasting" food that has none.

Some rather fascinating experiments were conducted with small children in relation to taste and eating. The children were allowed to eat all their meals cafeteria-style. There was a wide range of foods available, from meats and vegetables to fruits and sweets. The children ate whatever they wished for a period of months. Many mothers would predict that given such a choice children would eat nothing but sweets. Their prediction would be only partly correct. The children went on "food jags" during which they would indeed eat vast quantities of sweets. But they would also go on meat jags and vegetable jags. The children were repeatedly examined for any signs of malnutrition, as well as vitamin and mineral deficiency. There were no signs of malnutrition or any dietary deficiencies at the conclusion of the experiment. The children were able somehow to adjust their intake to obtain a completely balanced diet—all without vitamin pills and cajoling mothers! Surprisingly, the taste for sweets was over-ridden by some as yet unknown feedback mechanisms to the brain that directed the children's behavior in selecting more suitable foods.

Let us turn our attention to the means by which tissues receive their energy from the blood. Contained in blood plasma is the sugar glucose. This sugar is utilized by the cells of the body as an energy source. Measurement of blood sugar revealed that when people feel hunger, their blood-sugar level is low. When they are not hungry, their blood-sugar level is high. A brief look at the condition known as *diabetes* will help clarify the role of blood sugar in eating behavior.

The pancreas gland in a normal person releases a powerful chemical—*insulin*. This substance enables the tissues of the body to utilize blood sugar. Without insulin, blood sugar is not taken into the cells to be used but rather, remains in the blood, building up to very high levels. In diabetics, the pancreas is defective in its production of insulin, resulting in high blood-sugar levels (a common means of identifying diabetes) and tissue starvation. If diabetics are maintained by injections of insulin, they can lead relatively normal lives. If someone who is not hungry is given a dose of insulin, lowering the blood-sugar level, hunger will be experienced just as if he or she had gone for some time without eating. Thus, a drop in blood-sugar level is a stimulant to eat. Conversely, a high blood-sugar level reduces a person's appetite.

This later effect is the basis for a weight-reducing diet that requires eating a candy bar 30 minutes before meals, the argument being that the increase in blood sugar from eating the candy bar will reduce the appetite at mealtime. Unfortunately for fat people, the inhibitory effects of increased blood sugar are not as effective as the stimulating effects of the presence of food. The "candy-bar diet" is often ineffectual for weight reduction.

While activity pertaining to eating is widespread throughout the brain, most research has centered on the hypothalamus (see Figure 17). The anatomy of the hypothalamus is complex and its interconnections are diverse (see pages 57–58). We will consider only its basic operation. Research in the 1960s showed that there appear to be two regions of cells within the hypothalamus that are directly concerned with eating behavior. These cells are supplied with information regarding blood-sugar level, stomach contractions, taste and a host of other factors. One of the regions was thought to be a "stop eating" or satiety center. When a famished rat was electrically stimulated in this region, it ceased eating. The other area was considered to be a "start eating" or hunger center. A rat that was full proceeded to eat even more when stimulated here. The two centers were proposed to operate reciprocally, resulting in periods of feeding followed by periods of not eating. Such a system would function to maintain an adequate level of nutrients in an animal's body. This is another example of homeostasis, the maintenance of relatively constant conditions within the body.

According to this view the relationship between the two eating centers was one in which they complement one another, yet were opposed in function, with one center "starting" and the other center "stopping" eating. Such a relationship is also seen in the muscles of the body where one muscle (an extensor such as the triceps) works against another muscle (a flexor such as the biceps) to produce a precise movement. The relationship is termed a reciprocal one. Similar relationships are seen elsewhere in the brain.

As you might expect, a rat surgically deprived of its "start eating" center would not eat, even when very hungry and presented with its favorite food. If not force-fed, it would die of starvation. Similarly, a rat missing its "stop eating" center would overeat; in fact, it would continue to eat until it was two or three times its normal weight. This animal, although eating a prodigious amount, was actually quite particular about what it ate. If its food was mixed with bad-tasting substances, the rat would not eat the food. Its hunger seemed not to be general, but specific for good-tasting food. Further, it would not work very hard to obtain its food. A normal hungry rat will perform all sorts of tasks to obtain its ration. Not so for the rat with the hypothalamic "fat rat" syndrome. It would eat copiously only if obtaining the food required little or no expenditure of energy. The data gathered in the 1970s, however, require that this model be questioned on the following grounds: (1) destruction of other brain regions will produce a similar syndrome; (2) some of the effects are due to destruction of fibers passing through the hypothalamus, and (3) the effect of the lesions appears to involve influencing the "set point" for the amount of fat tissue an animal will maintain.

These observations of the "fat rat" bear a striking similarity to recent research on obesity conducted by Stanley Schacter. In a series of experiments done quite independently of the brain research on rats, he found that obese men and women eat more than persons whose weight is normal, but only if the food tastes good. Also, in an experiment in which normal and obese subjects were offered nuts in the shell at one time and shelled nuts at another, the fat subjects ate more only when the nuts were shelled. This evidence of obese subjects not being willing to exert much effort to obtain food was corroborated in restaurant observations. It was observed that overweight persons tend to choose foods that are easy to eat. For example, roast beef would be preferred over crab in the shell. In an Oriental restaurant whose customers were all Westerners, obese persons were more likely to eat with silverware rather than with the more difficult chopsticks.

Laboratory tests showed that although stomach contractions are a reliable indicator of desire to eat in a normal subject, this is not so for the obese. They are predisposed to eat both in the presence and in the absence of stomach contractions. Apparently they ignore the internal cues that guide the eating behavior of other persons. Schacter hypothesized that obese subjects were more under the control of external cues like odor and appearance and less under the control of internal events. To test this idea, overweight and normal subjects were given the task of proofreading a manuscript for errors. While they were engaged in that task, various disruptions were presented. True to prediction, the obese were more easily distracted than were the nonobese control subjects. The suggestion is that the obese have certain characteristics that contribute to their overeating and also function in behaviors that have nothing to do with eating. On the basis of this, we might suggest the ideal weight-reducing diet for the fat person.

The meals would consist of very difficult-to-eat foods served amidst much noise and commotion with the only utensils supplied being chopsticks!

Drinking

An explanation of drinking behavior is somewhat similar to that set forth for eating. An animal's tissues require an external supply of water, and the brain must detect this need and direct behavior for obtaining it. It is also possible for the tissues to be overloaded with water, and the brain must be able to direct elimination of an excess. The human body constantly loses water through breathing, sweating and the elimination of wastes. This water must be replaced. From eating, the body can conserve supplies of food as fat, but bodily reserves of water are scant indeed. A person can go without food for several months, but may die if deprived of water for only several days.

A decrease in body water lowers the amount of stored water surrounding the cells. Water contained in blood is used to replenish these stores. The blood, thus, loses water. The kidneys detect this decrease and secrete a chemical into the blood that is picked up by the hypothalamus. When thus activated, the hypothalamus directs the brain mechanisms that culminate in water-seeking behavior. As with eating behavior, the hypothalamus contains two discrete drinking areas: a "start drinking" area and a "stop drinking" one. Electrical or chemical stimulation of the appropriate center will result in the initiation or the cessation of drinking behavior. Surgical removal or "disconnection" of the appropriate area will produce an animal that will not drink or one that drinks to excess.

Sex

The survival and proliferation of a species depend upon many factors. Examples of two obvious ones are food supply and natural enemies. If, however, a species were incapable of reproducing itself, all the food in the world would not secure its survival. Thus, reproduction has a high rating in the scheme of life. It is no accident that mating behavior or sexual activity is one of the most pleasing and gratifying activities a human can engage in (it may be pleasurable to other animals as well, but such statements are only inferences). After all, if it were unpleasant, people would tend to refrain from sexual activity, which is obviously essential to the existence of the species.

Unlike eating and drinking, sexual activity does not satisfy a tissue need. Although people have been pictured as dying of a broken heart, no one has died as a result of sexual abstinence. Men and women can have quite adequate and full lives without ever engaging in sexual activity. Nonetheless, sexual behavior is a powerful source of human satisfaction and is thus important behavior.

Human sexual behavior is an enormously complex subject and to deal with it completely would require more space than is available in this book. Therefore, we shall limit our discussion to brain and hormonal influences on sexual behavior and especially to the sexual behavior of laboratory animals. The reader should be aware that research into sexual behavior and the discussion of sex (even from a medical point of view) is a rather recent phenomenon. Sexual activity has been around for quite some time, and people have indeed studied sexual behavior for most of this time. Yet, only recently has the study of sex been conducted with less personal interest and more scientific goals and methods.

In most animal species, the brain controls and regulates sexual behavior primarily by means of *hormones.* Primates are notable exceptions to this statement. Human sexual behavior depends more on personal experience and cultural molding than it does on hormones. A hormone is the chemical product of an endocrine gland. There are two general kinds of glands in the body. A gland such as a tear gland or a salivary gland that has a duct delivers its product through the duct to the target site (for example, the surface of the eye or the interior of the mouth). *Endocrine glands,* which are also called ductless glands, deposit their products—the hormones—into the bloodstream. The blood then carries the hormones to every part of the body. A hormone is often described as a substance that carries a "message" through the bloodstream. Some messages are excitatory and others are inhibitory. Of the two types of behavioral responses—hormonal and neural—the hormonal responses are much slower because they are transmitted by the relatively slow circulatory system. Some hormones such as the growth hormone act upon all of the tissues of the body. Other hormones are specific and cause a reaction in only one organ or at only one location; we call such an organ the target organ of the hormone. The hormonal transport mechanism is much the same as the luggage carrousel in airports. Each suitcase descends from a chute and travels around the carrousel, passing scores of "wrong targets" until its owner snatches it away.

We are discussing the endocrine system in order to understand what regulates sexual behavior. You should, of course, be aware that hormones exert control over many other types of behavior as well. As we shall see, the endocrine system and the nervous system interact so intimately to control sexual behavior that an argument might be made for considering them as parts of a single control system. Such intimate interaction between the two systems also functions in the regulation of the other behaviors that are affected by hormones.

The *pituitary* is the master endocrine gland. It releases a number of hormones, each of which performs a different job. The pituitary is termed the master gland because the targets of many of its hormones are other endocrine glands. Table 2 provides a summary of the pituitary hormones, their targets and their general functions. The mode of operation is relatively simple. The pituitary releases the hormone for a particular gland, which then picks up the hormone from the bloodstream and is roused into activity as a result of the "message" from the pitu-

Table 2 The pituitary hormones. Some of these stimulate production of other hormones.

Hormone	Target	Action
Growth hormone	Body tissues	Promotes growth
Thyrotrophic hormone	Thyroid gland	Stimulates production of thyroxin which regulates metabolic rate
Gonadotrophic hormone	Gonads	Stimulates production of gonadal hormones which influence sex behavior and characteristics
Adrenocorticotrophic hormone	Cortex of adrenal gland	Stimulates steroid production which controls water balance, metabolism
Lactogenic hormone	Mammary gland	Stimulates milk production
Oxytocin	Uterus	Stimulates uterine contractions
Vasopressin	Blood vessels	Stimulates vessel contraction, prevents fluid loss

itary. This gland then produces its own hormone and dumps it into the bloodstream where it, too, has a target (or targets) and an effect (or effects). As the second hormone is circulated by the blood to all parts of the body, the pituitary can sense how much of it is being produced and accordingly reduce or increase its hormone output. This is another example of feedback.

But what does the brain have to do with all of this? What is the "intimate interaction" between the endocrine system and the nervous system? The answer becomes apparent if we ask one more question: What regulates the pituitary?

The hypothalamus, located in the brain directly above the pituitary, is known to exert control over the pituitary by means of neural connections and chemical messengers. Some pituitary hormones are influenced by neural connections, others by chemical messengers. These chemical messengers, hormone-like substances that are called releasing factors, are the means by which the nervous system controls sexual behavior via the endocrine system.

The brain–endocrine control of sexual behavior thus begins when the hypothalamus secretes the appropriate releasing factor into the blood, which quickly reaches the pituitary and stimulates it to secrete *gonadotrophic hormone*. In the female the target gland of gonadotrophic hormone is the ovary. The ovary has two jobs to perform. First, it produces eggs, and second, it secretes hormones (*estrogen* and *progesterone*). The amount of ovarian hormones released is sensed by the pituitary, but this is far from being their sole function. Ovarian hormones are responsible for the development of secondary sexual characteristics that superficially distinguish females from males. In the human female such characteristics include the external structure of the genitals and the distribution of body fat and hair. In all mammals examined, gonadal hormones are responsible for brain dimorphisms (different structures) between males and females. There is no reason to expect the human brain to be different.

Most mammalian females, except the higher primates, display cycles in their sexual behavior. These cycles, called *estrous cycles,* are due to changes in the relative proportions of the two ovarian hormones. Only during a limited period within the cycle will the female accept the sexual advances of the male. The period of sexual receptivity, called estrus, or heat, is the period during which estrogen increases to its highest level. Sexual behavior in these animals is thus a result of a hormonal change. Because the ripening of eggs and their release for possible fertilization is regulated by this same hormonal cycle, the overall effect is to concentrate sexual activity in the period during which the likelihood of conception is greatest.

The human female exhibits only slight cyclical sexual behavior. Ovarian hormones (and eggs) are produced in a regular cycle, but this has little effect on behavior. The sexual behavior of human beings is based primarily on past experiences and cultural influences. Still, alterations in hormonal level such as those that occur when women experience menopause (a gradual cessation of ovarian hormone production) can temporarily disrupt sexual behavior.

In the male the target gland of the gonadotrophic hormone is the testis. Like the ovary, the testis has a dual role: sperm production and hormone production. *Androgens,* the hormones released by the testis, are different from the female hormones, but the general effects are the same. Pituitary hormones stimulate the production of testicular hormones, which, in turn, regulate the production of pituitary hormones by means of feedback. Androgens are also responsible for the development of secondary sexual characteristics and, in nonprimates, sexual behavior (Figure 36). In short, there are basic similarities in male and female hormone production, although the hormones produced are different.

The hypothalamus shapes sexual behavior in another way in addition to its interaction with the endocrine system. In many animals it is the origin of direct neural effects such as mounting behaviors. In this case hormones are not involved.

A good deal is known about sexual behavior and how it is regulated in laboratory animals. Considerably less is known about other animals and humans. There is no doubt a good deal of overlap, however. One of the most fruitful ways to consider the brain–endocrine control of sexual behavior is to examine the effects of various laboratory manipulations on rodents. Rats that are not yet sexually mature do not have adult levels of pituitary sex hormones circulating in their bloodstreams. As the pituitary sex hormone level is low, the ovaries or testes of young rats are not active in an adult manner.

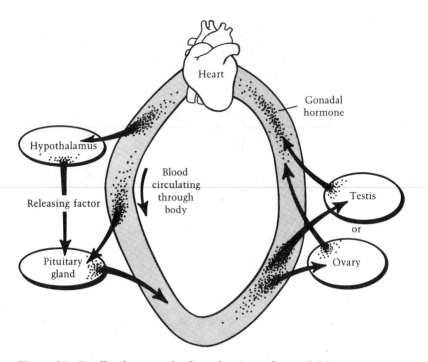

Figure 36 Feedback control of production of gonadal hormones. The hypothalamus causes the pituitary gland to release hormone into the blood that is circulating through the body. This hormone is picked up by the ovary or the testis, which is thereby stimulated to release a gonadal hormone into the bloodstream. The gonadal hormone is detected by the pituitary and the hypothalamus, which are thereby inhibited from releasing more pituitary hormone.

If female hormones are administered to an immature male rat, the animal will display adult female sexual behaviors. These behaviors include the retrieval of young and stereotyped female postures. If male hormones are given to an immature male, adult male sex behaviors are observed. Thus, the behavior of the immature rat may be altered by hormones (see Table 3).

Hormonal manipulation has also been attempted on adult animals, whose pituitaries are producing gonadotrophic hormones and whose gonads have developed. Administration of female hormones to an adult male does not produce characteristic female sexual behaviors. In fact, the

Table 3 The effects of hormonal treatment upon the sexual behavior of laboratory rats.

Subjects	Treatment	Behavior
Immature rats	None	No sexual behavior
	Given androgens	Adult male sexual behavior
	Given estrogens	Adult female sexual behavior
Mature rats	None	Adult male sexual behavior
	Given androgens	Adult male sexual behavior
	Given estrogens	Adult male sexual behavior
Mature rats castrated when mature	None	No sexual behavior
	Given androgens	Adult male sexual behavior
	Given estrogens	Adult female sexual behavior
Mature rats castrated	None	Gradual decline in adult male sexual behavior
	Given androgens	Maintains or reestablishes adult male sexual behavior
	Given estrogens	Gradual decline in adult male sexual behavior

behavior of the animals does not change much, if at all. If male hormones are administered to an adult male, the result is again minimal. Thus, it appears that once the pituitary comes into play at puberty, hormonal injections have little or no effect.

It is known that there is a crucial period in a developing embryo regarding the development of sexual organs. Up to a certain stage, mammalian embryos have the capacity to become either male or female depending on pituitary (and in turn brain) activity. Normally, the pituitary hormones are genetically controlled and bring about development of the sex that was determined at conception. Pituitary activity can be interfered with experimentally, permitting change in the sex of a developing animal almost at will. After the critical development stage has passed, however, it is impossible to alter the course of sexual development in any major way.

You might expect that if rats were deprived of pituitary sex hormones throughout their lives, they would be rather asexual. Removal of the pituitary for experimental purposes is not a possibility because it governs so many other vital functions. The next best thing for the investigation we are interested in is to remove the gonads upon which the pituitary acts. A castrated immature rat will not develop sexual behaviors because he has no gonadal hormones. If, however, he is administered male hormones as an adult, he will display adult male sexual behavior. If he is administered female hormones, his behavior will be female. Thus, this animal, like the immature rat, has proved to be susceptible to hormonal molding of sexual behavior. If injections of male hormone are given regularly, he can perform the sexual behaviors of a normal male (mounting and so on) but obviously cannot father rat pups because he is lacking in sperm-production machinery.

The story for a male rat that is castrated after reaching sexual maturity is somewhat more complex. His male sexual behavior will slowly decline with time. If, however, he has had a lot of experience in sexual matters, his old behavior patterns may die more slowly than would a rat's who had abstained. The sexual behaviors of a castrated adult can be restored by administration of male hormone. The effect of castration on adult humans is even more dependent upon experience. In fact, it is usually impossible to detect any difference in sexual behavior for years following castration.

Vasectomy, which is simple to perform in humans, is the surgical removal of a part of the vas deferens, the structure that carries the sperm from the testes to the penis. This operation, which is performed as a means of birth control, should not be confused with castration. The testes remain to act as glands, and still respond to pituitary commands to secrete testicular hormones. Thus, possible side effects of castration do not accompany this operation.

≡ Summary

≡ *In this section we have examined brain mechanisms that control certain behaviors. There are, for example, a number of influences that work together to determine whether an animal will start or stop eating. These influences include stomach contractions, taste of food and blood-sugar level. We have seen that one part of the brain, the hypothalamus, is intimately involved in the regulation of eating behaviors.*

The control of drinking behavior is under similar hypothalamic control. The hypothalamus monitors the amount of water in the body and directs behavior to maintain the required amount.

Sexual behavior is similarly under brain control. In addition to purely neural control, sexual behavior is under the regulation of hormonal influences as well. Particularly with animals other than the primates, the hormonal levels in the blood determine sexual behavior. The pituitary and the hypothalamus interact as a two-part control system, with feedback being an essential mechanism in the system. The physical development of the gonads in both humans and lower animals is under the brain-directed control of the pituitary. Once the pituitary establishes control, it is impossible to alter the physical aspect of sexuality or to change sexual behavior appreciably. Injected sex hormones can elicit sexual behavior in rats, but in humans, the manipulation of sex hormones produces less apparent effects because human sexual behavior is determined primarily by past experience rather than by hormonal levels.

Suggestions for Further Reading

The Brain. San Francisco: W. H. Freeman, 1979.

Eccles, J. "The Synapse." *Scientific American,* January 1965. (Offprint 1001)

Evarts, E. V. "Brain Mechanisms in Movement." *Scientific American,* July 1973. (Offprint 1277)

Fisher, A. E. "Chemical Stimulation of the Brain." *Scientific American,* June 1964. (Offprint 485)

Gregory, R. L. *Eye and Brain.* New York: McGraw-Hill, 1966.

Guillemin, R., and Burgus, R. "The Hormones of the Hypothalamus. *Scientific American,* November 1972. (Offprint 1260)

Heimer, L. "Pathways in the Brain." *Scientific American,* July 1971. (Offprint 1227)

Hubel, D. H. "The Visual Cortex of the Brain." *Scientific American,* November 1963. (Offprint 168)

Kandel, E. R. "Nerve Cells and Behavior." *Scientific American,* July 1970. (Offprint 1182)

Katz, B. "How Cells Communicate." *Scientific American,* September 1961. (Offprint 98)

Levine, S. "Sex Differences in the Brain." *Scientific American,* April 1966. (Offprint 498)

Merton, P. A. "How We Control the Contraction of Our Muscles." *Scientific American,* May 1972. (Offprint 1249)

Michael, C. R. "Retinal Processing of Visual Images." *Scientific American,* May 1969. (Offprint 1143)

Miller, W. H.; Ratliff, F.; and Hartline, H. K. "How Cells Receive Stimuli." *Scientific American,* September 1961. (Offprint 99)

Pettigrew, J. D. "The Neurophysiology of Binocular Vision." *Scientific American,* August 1972. (Offprint 1255)

Pritchard, R. M. "Stabilized Images on the Retina." *Scientific American,* June 1961. (Offprint 466)

Stent, G. S. "Cellular Communication." *Scientific American,* September 1972. (Offprint 1257)

Thompson, R. F. *Physiological Psychology.* San Francisco: W. H. Freeman, 1972.

von Békésy, G. "The Ear." *Scientific American,* August 1957. (Offprint 44)

3
Brain and Behavior

In this section we shall discuss several important topics that are being actively investigated in the brain sciences. Some of the topics concern normal processes that take place in living animals. Others concern external influences that, being brought to bear on the brain, alter it and thus alter behavior as well. Some common social problems such as drug abuse are involved among the latter topics. Some of the external influences such as the electrical stimulation of the brain by means of electrodes implanted deep within the brain are rather unusual (except in science fiction).

Early Experiences

In the preceding chapter (pages 75–77), we saw that the visual cortex of a cat's brain was essentially "prewired." The responses of individual neurons in a newborn kitten are similar to those in an adult cat. From this and other evidence it was deduced that much of the brain is "ready to use" and does not depend on experience to make it operative. This does not mean, however, that the environment of an animal or human has no effect on the brain. Far from it—the environment profoundly affects the brain, especially the brain of a growing and developing animal. During its development the brain is most susceptible to change—change that may be brought about by environmental events.

A developing animal must have some contact with the visual world. Without visual experiences the elegant prewiring of the visual cortex will be for nought—the fine and intricate structure will break down and the potential visual ability will deteriorate. We may assume that the same ground rules hold for other brain systems: Direct experience of the environment is necessary for both development and maintenance of the sensory cortex. Thus, although organisms are "given" a functioning sensory analyzer, they must interact with the environment to prevent deterioration of this equipment and to develop its potential to the full. The implication is clear—if you don't use it, you'll lose it!

Even as deprivation of visual experience can affect the basic neural organization, so can less severe alterations in the environment, although, of course, with less severe effects. A convincing example is provided by experiments in which people wore special goggles that distorted vision. The simplest distortion merely displaced the visual field by 5 to 10 degrees (Figure 37). The effect was that an object at arm's length viewed as being "dead ahead" was actually located 6 or 8 inches to one side. As you might expect, this made it difficult for the wearer to move through space. It took only a few hours' experience, however, for the wearer to become perfectly accustomed to the displacement.

A more drastic distortion was produced by goggles that inverted the visual world. Here too there was an initial period of confusion and disorientation. But after a few days, the wearer was so at ease with his topsy-turvy world

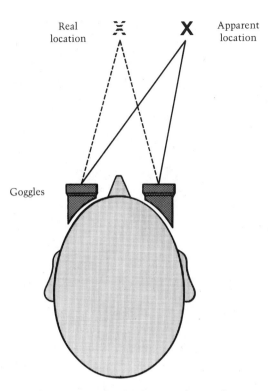

Figure 37 An experiment in which special goggles were worn that visually displaced objects in the environment. The wearers adjusted rather quickly to minor spatial displacements as well as to a completely upside-down world.

that he could successfully navigate a bicycle down a crowded street! So accustomed had the subject become to his upside-down world that when the goggles were removed, and his vision was "normal" again, he reported that the image of the world was upside-down again! Obviously, the human brain is capable of adjusting to such environmental changes as a visual inversion. Not all animals are endowed with such a versatile brain—newly hatched chicks fitted with goggles that displace the visual world will, unlike humans, never adjust to the displacement and will continue to peck where they "see" the grain.

These changes in the brain due to alteration in the visual world caused by wearing the goggles are temporary, short-term solutions devised to meet specific problems. The brain produces other types of solutions that seem to depend upon wired-in, or innate, perceptions—relating, for example, to the fear of depth—that apparently function throughout life. Experiments using the *visual cliff* have demonstrated the universality of this aversion. If an infant is placed on an apparatus like the one in Figure 38, which has a thick glass surface with a pattern design several feet beneath the glass on the other side, he or she will consistently avoid the "deep" side. Also, ani-

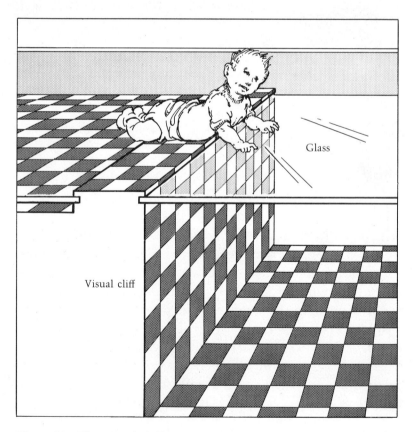

Figure 38 The visual cliff.

mals as diverse as lambs, chicks and children will scurry out of the "deep" side if placed on the glass over it, even though they can feel the solid glass under their bodies!

Other experiments performed on cats offer even more dramatic proof of the modifiability of the brain. Adult cats were reared either in an environment enclosed by a surface on which were painted horizontal stripes or in one with vertical stripes. Some time later the cats were tested for evidence of an alteration in the visual region of the brain. The results were clear. The neurons in the visual cortex of these cats responded predominantly to the orientation of the stripes to which they were exposed earlier. For example, a cat exposed to horizontal stripes had many more neurons that responded to horizontal lines than to vertical lines. Furthermore, its behavior suggested that it was functionally blind to a stick held vertically, yet perfectly able to see and respond to the same stick held horizontally.

The results of these experiments are quite illuminating: They suggest that, through manipulation of the environment, we can alter the brain itself. Nevertheless, we cannot be sure that the matter of the brain was actually altered in the sense of having one kind of patterning in it replaced by another. It could be, for example, that neurons in the "vertical" cats that normally respond to horizontality have died rather than being transformed into neurons that respond to verticality.

≡ Summary

We have seen that the brain is a complex structure whose blueprint is laid down in the genetic code of an animal. This is not to say that the environment has no effect on the developing brain or on its ultimate function. Indeed, the environment plays a significant role in determining both the nature of the brain and behavior. In this section we have seen several examples of how the environment profoundly affects the brain. Environmental effects are especially pronounced on a developing brain. Many experiments have shown that interactions of the environment with the brain can produce profound changes in brain function itself. In summary, we can say that although an animal inherits a brain based on a genetic blueprint, its final form and function is determined by interactions with the environment.

Rhythms of Life

As much as some individuals would like to deny it, we are nevertheless very much creatures of habit. We exhibit variations in body temperature and blood-sugar levels throughout the day. Males and females exhibit daily variation in hormonal levels that can be quite predictable. All of these physiologic states are cyclic, that is, they recur on a regular basis. The term given for such cyclic behaviors is circadian, which refers to a 24-hour periodicity for most of these rhythms.

It is important to distinguish *circadian rhythms* from those alterations in behavior and state that are driven by events in the environment. Many of the things that we do on a periodic basis are not truly circadian. To qualify as a circadian rhythm, the phenomenon must reoccur at roughly its same rate in the total absence of external influences. For example, an individual maintained under conditions of constant darkness (as in a cave) for an extended time period will develop waking and sleep patterns which differ only slightly from the twenty-four-hour day.

Given this definition of circadian rhythms, we can exclude such environmentally triggered phenomena as eating at certain times of the day and certain patterns of physical activity. Left as truly circadian rhythms are variations in body temperature, blood-glucose levels, hormonal levels, sleep and certain electroencephalogram (EEG) rhythms. Since all of these phenomena can occur in the absence of environmental stimuli, it suggests that there exists a biological "clock" that governs the appearance of these phenomena.

For many circadian rhythms, it has been determined that a nucleus in the hypothalamus, the superchiasmatic nucleus, serves as a pacemaker to organize all of the circadian rhythms of the body. The superchiasmatic nucleus itself is apparently not the clock; it only synchronizes many of the clocks located in various organs. For example, the adrenal cortex will continue to secrete hormones on a cyclic basis in the total absence of either environmental cues or the superchiasmatic nucleus. The hypothalamic pacemaker serves only to coordinate the rhythmic activities of the various pacemaker cells located in different tissues.

Circadian rhythms are a common phenomena in most forms of animal and plant life. An understanding of the functional importance and utility of these circadian rhythms in conjunction with the behavioral relevance of these phenomena should yield great insight into the nature of brain/behavior interaction and control of behavioral state.

Nature–Nurture

For many years it was alternately fashionable to argue that the major determinant of a child's personality was (1) innate (the nature argument) or (2) learned (the nurture argument). These approaches ignored the fact that neither innate nor learned factors operate in a vacuum upon development. Each requires the other. The only reasonable question is "What is the interaction between nature and nurture?" A logical means of investigating this question is to hold nature constant and vary nurture. A difficulty arises in holding nature constant, however, in studies of human beings—controlled-breeding experiments are not a possibility! It is therefore helpful to use other animals in experiments designed to determine the general principles governing the interaction between nature and nurture. The laboratory rat, which has been in-bred for many generations, is a particularly good subject for such experiments because a great deal is known about its genetic history.

In a series of experiments conducted at the University of California, Berkeley, brain scientists constructed an elaborate "kindergarten" for laboratory rats (Figure 39). The purpose was to answer the critical question as to the degree to which the environment can interact with and alter the basic structure of the brain. The strategy employed was to provide rats that were littermates with different degrees of "environmental enrichment." Littermates were used in order to keep differences due to genetics to a minimum. Some of the littermates were kept socially isolated, that is, one to a cage with the cages far enough apart to prevent social interaction. This group of rats was what scientists call a *control group*. These animals were used as comparisons for animals reared in the enriched environment. The "enrichment" comprised social interaction with their peers plus the availability of toys carefully chosen to gladden the heart of any young rat. On reaching a certain age, the rats were given the rat equivalent of an IQ test. Upon close examination it was discovered that rats from an enriched environment had a markedly "superior" brain as determined by a number of measures. The neocortex of the "enriched" rats was thicker, suggesting that the neurons, which had not increased in number, had formed a more complex net of interconnections.

The Berkeley scientists also discovered that the enriched rats had greater amounts of several important brain chemicals and surpassed the other rats according to a variety of other measures of brain growth and development. Not surprisingly, these rats also did better on the IQ test than did the relatively impoverished littermates. The test was a discrimination-reversal problem for which the rats had to reverse a previously learned response of approaching one stimulus and avoiding another. These studies demonstrated the potential of the brain to grow and de-

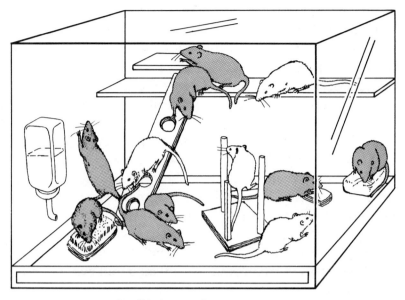

Rat "kindergarten"

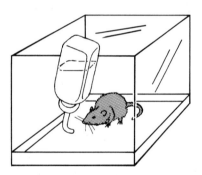

Impoverished environment

Figure 39 Living in an enriched or impoverished environment.

velop in a rich environment. They were used in a success-ful campaign for enactment of social legislation to aid the children of the disadvantaged.

Harry Harlow, a scientist at the University of Wis-consin, also studied the relationship between nature and nurture—not in the context of brain growth and environ-mental complexity, but rather, in regard to the factors governing "mother love." Harlow's experimental subjects were monkeys. For some time it had been fashionable to consider that the affection for mother readily exhibited by humans and many other animals was due to a learned dependency. That is, a helpless infant received life-giving food from its mother, and thus was positively reinforced for approaching and clinging to its mother by the alleviation of hunger. This view was dealt a deathblow by the work of Harlow.

What Harlow did was to capitalize on the observation that infant monkeys become very attached to pieces of cloth placed in their cages. They become acutely distressed if their "security blankets" are removed even for short periods. Harlow theorized, correctly as we shall see later, that physical contact was a prime moving force in the development of the mother-child bond of affection. The experiment used two groups of infant monkeys. Each of the monkeys was placed in a special cage that contained two "surrogate" mothers. One of the surrogate mothers, as shown in Figure 40, was constructed of bare wire and the other of wire covered with soft terrycloth. Depending upon which group an infant monkey was in, it received its milk from a nipple protruding from either the wire or cloth mother's "breast." Harlow simply noted with which of the two surrogate mothers the infants spent time. Those people favoring a learned-dependency explanation of mother love would, of course, predict that the monkeys would prefer whichever surrogate mother supplied them with milk. However, had these persons wagered on the outcome of the experiment, they would have emerged poorer. All of the monkeys, as is shown in Figure 41, preferred the cloth mother, even those that received their milk from the wire mother. Harlow termed the binding force between the infants and their cloth mothers *contact comfort*. To paraphrase Harlow concerning the controversy: If learned dependencies are to be invoked as an explanation of the monkey's behavior, the dependency must be fashioned from whole cloth rather than whole milk.

Harlow went on to show that other factors also enter into an infant's preference among surrogate mothers.

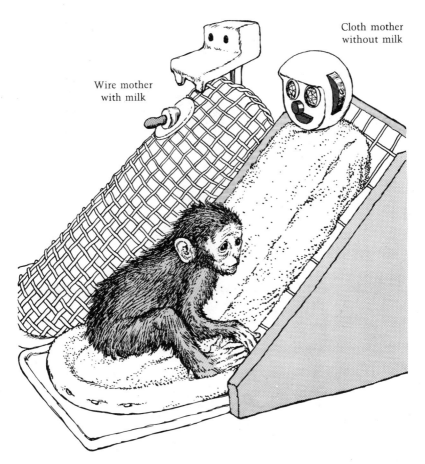

Wire mother
with milk

Cloth mother
without milk

Figure 40 Cloth and wire surrogate mothers.

For example, a warm cloth mother is preferred over a cool
one and a rocking mother is preferred over a still one. That
the infant monkeys really felt that the surrogates were
mothers was demonstrated rather convincingly by a variety of further demonstrations. At one point the infants
were placed into small rooms with objects, such as rattles,
plastic "creatures," and other children's toys, that seemed
to be frightening to the monkeys. If the surrogate mothers
were also in the room, the infant would immediately rush
to the cloth mother for protection and comfort. Only after
clinging for awhile to the cloth surrogate would the infant
begin to explore the new territory.

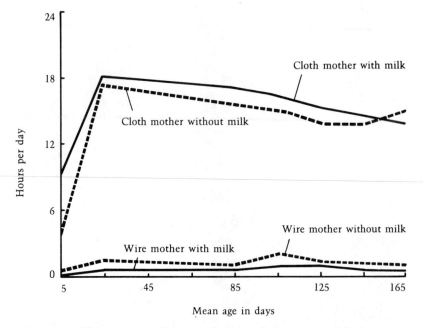

Figure 41 The amount of time infant monkeys spent with the cloth mother or with the wire mother. The presence or absence of food associated with the surrogate mothers made little difference in the animals' behavior toward them. (Adapted from "Love in Infant Monkeys" by H. F. Harlow. Copyright 1959 by Scientific American, Inc. All rights reserved.)

If, however, the cloth mother was absent from the room, the infant would freeze in terror until removed. Thus, we can see that contact comfort, at least for the monkey, is the most important determinant in its recognition of a "mother."

The brain is an exquisitely complex organ. This complexity is determined partly by genetic inheritance and partly by interactions with the environment. Behavior, in turn, is under the control of the brain and thus shaped by both nature and nurture. Scientists are now beginning to unravel the brain mechanisms underlying behavior. It can be expected that in the years to come neuroscientists will understand more clearly the interplay between the two components. The identification of genetic and environmental influences on brain function (and thus on behavior) may allow us to eliminate negative influences and enhance positive ones. Such knowledge, properly applied, might do much to improve the human condition.

≡ Summary

In this section we examined the nature–nurture issue and saw the important question: What is the interaction between nature and nurture? Although it is easy to pose the question in this manner, it is not necessarily easy to perform the appropriate experiments to answer it because genetic and environmental factors cannot always be controlled. Several strategies have been reviewed here, including the use of the inbred laboratory rat. It was shown that laboratory rats exposed to an enriched environment actually develop changes in the basic structure of the brain. The nature–nurture question was viewed from the aspect of mother-child relationships in monkeys. For a long time, it had been believed that the bond between mother and child was formed as a result of the infant's receiving nourishment from the mother. The experiments with monkeys invalidated this belief. They showed that the receipt of food from a "mother" was not the important factor in determining an infant's attachment to her; rather, the provision of a soft surface to which the infant could cling was the important factor.

≡ *The Plastic Brain*

≡ It is hard to imagine what behavior would be like if suddenly we were all incapable of learning new information or remembering past events. We would not be able to navigate in space because we would not remember the meaning or significance of the objects we see. Indeed, we would not even recognize and be able to identify common things in the environment such as buildings, trees and cars. Furthermore, we would be unable to adjust to this memory problem because we would be unable to learn anything new about our environment. We would be reduced to existing in the here and now without recourse to language, reflection or planning for the future. All sensory stimuli would be totally devoid of meaning. Such common and pleasurable phenomena as music and sports would appear as nonsense to us. So all-important are the abilities to learn and remember that we often forget how critical and essential they are to our normal daily activities.

To what extent is the brain involved in learning and memory? In a very real sense, one can consider that the central nervous system is an organ of the body that is specialized for the processing of information. In the human being, and in other complicated animals, a large part of the processing that goes on in the brain is concerned with the understanding of the world around us with respect to our personal history. Think of yourself this very moment. You are reading a textbook which requires that you have a mastery of the English language and know how to read. Thus, this activity depends upon many years of interaction with English-speaking people plus the formal education that you have had in school. In addition, you are (hopefully) remembering the things that you have read in previous paragraphs and sections in this book and know the reason for studying this particular book. Perhaps you are taking a course that requires that you read this book or perhaps you are reading it outside of the formal demands of a classroom. In any event, the words that you are reading now have meaning only in the context of the previous words that have appeared on the pages of this book. Furthermore, the language in this book is evoking in your mind specific images which relate to commonly held experiences. For example, several sentences ago reference was made to trees and cars. Clearly, an attribute of language is that it ascribes common terms to things in the environment that we all have familiarity with, such that communication between individuals is possible. Thus, all of these things and more are occurring simultaneously while you are in the process of reading this paragraph. Without the operation of learning and memory, none of this would be possible.

Let us for a moment separate learning from memory. In reality, of course, the two are firmly intermeshed. If, for example, you were to be deprived of your ability to learn for the next few minutes, what would be the consequences of this on your behavior? Would you still be able to read these sentences? Yes, the language learning that you have accomplished occurred some time ago (unless you are a new speaker of English) and now resides in your long-term memory. Deprived of your ability to learn, you would still have access to this stored memory. Brain and behavior scientists have identified two phases of memory—a long-term and a short-term phase. The ability to recall a telephone number for a few minutes, the ability to paraphrase the last paragraph you read and repeat it a few moments later, these are forms of short-term memory that may or may not rely on a long-term or permanent stored memory in order for them to be performed. However, they do require learning. Without the ability to understand the new relationships between words that are presented in this paragraph, it would be impossible for you to form short-term or long-term memories. Therefore, without the ability to learn of new events in the environment, you cannot form new memories.

If, however, you were temporarily impaired in your ability to utilize short-term memory, then the material that you learned in the previous paragraph would be immediately forgotten. In fact, from sentence to sentence you would forget the content of the previous sentence. Obviously, in such a situation, what you were reading would be totally meaningless because it would not appear in context.

If you were deprived of long-term memory, the results would be quite different. With this temporary problem, you would be able to read and understand the contents of this book or the rules for playing a game, or anything else; however, you would not be able to use that information at a later time. If someone were to meet you for the first time while you were suffering from an impairment in long-term memory, you could learn the name of that person and remember it for awhile, yet if that individual came to you a day later, you would have absolutely no recollection of ever having met him or her before.

Again, back to a fundamental question: What does the brain have to do with all of this? While we are very far from understanding how the brain learns and stores information, we do have some clues as to the operation of this fundamental process. We know that lesions to a portion of the limbic system of the brain, the hippocampus, will result in an individual that is unable to form long-term memories. The classical case of a patient known only as H. M. illustrates this quite well. H. M. can learn new material and can repeat it quite well for several minutes. However, if queried on subsequent days about what it was he had learned, he has absolutely no knowledge of his earlier learning. As you can imagine, this can be a severe handicap to normal daily activities. H. M., for example, moved from his home to another shortly after his hippocampal operation. In the months and years that followed that move, H. M. was never able to remember that he did not live at his old location and was repeatedly found heading toward his previous home. Similarly, although he was treated by the same set of physicians on an almost daily basis for years, he never learned their names or identities. To him they were always strangers. Clearly, someone without access to long-term memory stores is a severely handicapped individual. Fortunately there are few natural occurrences of difficulties with long-term memory. Severe alcoholism can damage structures in the brain that are connected to the hippocampus and result in impairments of long-term memory functioning.

There are no known cases of individuals *incapable* of learning. Certainly there are many unfortunate examples of individuals impaired in their ability to learn. Many children are born with genetic defects such as Downs Syndrome, which leave them mentally retarded and capable of functioning only at very elementary levels. These individuals are seriously impaired in their ability to learn and remember. We do not know, however, what in the brain has actually gone awry to result in this condition. Similarly, defects in short-term memory are difficult to dissociate from defects in learning or long-term memory. Short-term memory is generally not tested in our formalized educational system, only long-term memory is generally examined and as one can understand, long-term memory is the ultimate consequence of (1) learning and (2) short-term memory. Therefore, difficulty in long-term memory may, in fact, reflect difficulties in either learning, short-term memory or long-term memory.

Since we know that the operation of the brain depends upon synaptic connections between millions of neurons, it is not unreasonable to assume that it is these elements that are somehow involved in learning and memory. An early theory of learning was proposed by Professor Donald Hebb, a Canadian brain scientist. Professor Hebb reasoned that the electrical activity that is seen to be occurring at all times in the central nervous system may form the basis for short-term information storage in the brain. He reasoned that once a pattern of electrical activity representing some event or process is established in the brain, if that electrical event were to continue to circle about or reverberate through the myriad brain circuits available, this might provide a means of storing that information for a period of time.

Long-term storage of information in the brain probably does not use reverberatory neural activity as a storage mechanism. Consider, if you will, that you will still possess many memories that you currently hold when you are scores of years older. What sort of biological mechanism can hold information over spans of decades? Most people thinking of the brain mechanism for storing information for such extended periods of time, have, by a process of default, come to the position that there must be a structural change in the nervous system that underlies that storage. By structural change is meant either an alteration in the connections between neurons or a microscopic change in the features of the connections that already exist.

Before discussing the details of neuronal information storage, let us consider for a moment what form that information might take as it is being processed by the central nervous system. When looking at an automobile for example, the image of that vehicle is influencing the activity of millions of photoreceptors on the retina. These cells, in turn, send information back through the thalamus and project to the visual cortex and other regions of the neocortex where the brain perceives that the image being looked at is an automobile.

One way of storing this neural representation of the automobile is to permanently change all of those synapses throughout the pathways just activated. Two considerations are important with respect to this means of storage. First, a widespread pattern change must be accomplished to store this image and, secondly, a widespread alteration of the brain in storing the features of the automobile might interfere with the storage of features of other objects to be encountered in the future. In consideration of the latter point, many believe that only certain regions in the brain are designed to store information, whereas other areas are designed to process sensory information, for example. Most would believe that there must be a distributed form of information storage which will allow the millions of neural elements that become involved in even the simplest of perceptions to store that information over periods of time.

Returning to our two mechanisms of information storage in the brain—that of altered connectivity or altered efficacy of existing connectivity—let us consider these two alternatives further. It is certainly conceivable that new connections can be grown within the central nervous system to allow for the encoding of information. Most neurons of the central nervous system do not further divide after birth, yet the brain continues to grow in volume. Most of this growth in volume is accomplished not by the addition of new cells, but rather by the growth of new connections between existing cells. It is now known that this growth of connections continues throughout life.

Short-term memory is a temporary thing. Not until information has been placed in long-term storage is it relatively permanent and relatively immune to easy disruption. It is not inconceivable that the time that is necessary for long-term memory establishment represents the time that is required to grow new connections between elements in the brain. Major reorganizations are not occurring within the brain when one learns something. Students do not grow new fiber tracts spanning from one side of the brain to the other. Rather, what might be happening is that very tiny changes are occurring in the vicinity of nerve cells. What is changing are the details of the connections, rather than the overall structure of the brain. We know, for example, that an animal placed in an environment that contains interesting objects and learning potentialities will develop a brain that is richer in connections than will an animal placed in a plain laboratory cage. These facts support the theory that the permanent registration of information in the brain is accompanied by a pattern of altered connections.

The alternative mechanism for storing information for long periods of time in the central nervous system involves not the growth of new connections, but rather the alteration of existing ones. Clearly, if one alters an existing connection (either strengthening it or weakening it), such a mechanism could underlie long-term information storage. In a previous example a certain array of synapses was used to represent an automobile. If it were possible to strengthen those synapses, such that the next time that car were seen it would travel that pathway with greater facility, then this would be a means of storing that information. A modulation in the effectiveness of synaptic coupling or efficacy is a second way that the brain may have of storing information for relatively long periods of time.

The perceptive reader will recognize that these changes in synaptic efficacy may also involve structural changes in the nervous system. For example, one way of making a synaptic connection more effective would be to place more receptors onto the recipient cell. A given amount of neurotransmitters released would have a greater effect on the recipient cell given more receptors. Clearly, the addition of new receptors is a structural change, albeit at a molecular level.

There are many ways in which the nervous system could effect changes in synaptic efficacy. In addition to growing new receptors, a neuron could release more neurotransmitter, could less efficiently deactivate released transmitter, could more effectively make use of the synaptic signal, or it could recruit as yet unappreciated mechanisms to account for increased synaptic efficacy.

In recent years, brain scientists have uncovered an interesting candidate mechanism that might underlie long-term information storage in the brain. This phenomenon, termed *long-term potentiation* (LTP), is seen at the synapses between neurons in the hippocampus and other regions of the brain. LTP is an enduring change in synaptic efficacy that is produced by a certain pattern of activation of the synapse under study. The elevation in synaptic efficacy more than doubles. That is, after being appropriately activated, the output of the synapse is more than double what it was prior to activation. LTP lasts for a very long time, up to weeks or months in suitable preparations.

LTP has the characteristics required of a neural system that can underlie some, if not all, of the aspects of information storage in the brain. Interestingly, LTP has been studied most extensively not in the intact brains of laboratory animals, but rather in a new development in the brain sciences—the brain-slice preparation. In the preparation, a small portion of brain tissue is removed from the animal and placed in a specially constructed chamber which serves to duplicate the conditions found in the brain itself. The tissue can be kept alive for periods up to 10 hours and studied electrically, chemically or anatomically while in this tissue chamber. The great advantage of the brain-slice technique is that all of the confounding and confusing activity in the rest of the brain which often makes the interpretation of results difficult is, of course, removed.

In the 1950s, brain scientists were exploring only tentatively the brain mechanisms that might underlie learning and memory. By the 1980s, this tentative exploration had been supplanted by a firm commitment to understanding the neural mechanisms underlying learning and memory. Furthermore, the discovery of potential neural mechanisms of learning and memory such as long-term potentiation has created a feeling that the great mystery of the brain mechanisms of learning and memory will be solved in the forseeable future.

≡ Summary
≡
≡ *Neuronal plasticity is a term given to those neuronal phenomena that underlie learning and memory. Learning and memory are essential qualities which when impaired leave a profound impact on the sufferer. Memory is divided into a short-term and a long-term phase. The short-term phase of memory is capable of being interrupted, whereas the long-term phase of memory is more resistent to interference. The process of converting short-term into long-term memory is termed memory consolidation.*

The brain correlates of learning and memory are currently under intensive investigation. It has been suggested that short-term memory is represented in the brain by the electrical activity of neurons connected together in circuits. Such reverberating neural activity would be sufficient to encode experience. The long-term phase of memory is most probably represented by a change in the physical makeup of the central nervous system. That change may be represented in the form of alterations in existing connections between the brain cells or in the appearance of new patterns of connections between neurons involved in information storage. A recent candidate for long-term information storage in the brain has been discovered in the hippocampus. This phenomenon known as long-term potentiation is an enduring change in the way that neurons communicate with one another.

Electrical Activity of the Brain

The brain is not an electric machine; it does not run on electricity, nor does it generate much electricity (something on the order of a few millionths of a volt at the surface of the brain). It is a biochemical machine; it runs on metabolic substances and conducts its business by electrochemical means (see pages 36–44). Nevertheless, the electricity generated as a by-product of the electrochemical events can be measured and the measurements so obtained permit scientists to examine the more basic electrochemistry. Physicians don't often open the chest to observe the heart; they rely upon listening to the heart sounds with a stethoscope. They have learned that the various sounds signify different events and conditions. Analogously, brain scientists have learned about the relations between a recording of the electrical activity in the brain and the underlying electrochemical events.

There are two ways to record the electrical activity of the brain. The first and most common is to place metal disc electrodes on the surface of the scalp and record the electrical activity of the brain beneath. The very weak signals are amplified and recorded on a moving paper. The graphic record is an *electroencephalogram* (EEG). Figure 42 shows a diagram of the recording instrument, which is called an electroencephalograph. Electrodes can be placed over many different brain areas and an EEG can then be made of the activity of countless millions of brain cells acting, more or less, together.

To the uninitiated, the EEG appears to be a meaningless collection of squiggly lines. However, study reveals consistent patterns in EEGs and relationships between certain patterns and various behavioral states. Figure 43 dramatically demonstrates what happens to the EEG when a relaxed person closes his or her eyes. The most profound changes in EEG take place as a person progresses from the fully awake, alert state into deep sleep. The EEG of an awake, alert person is characterized

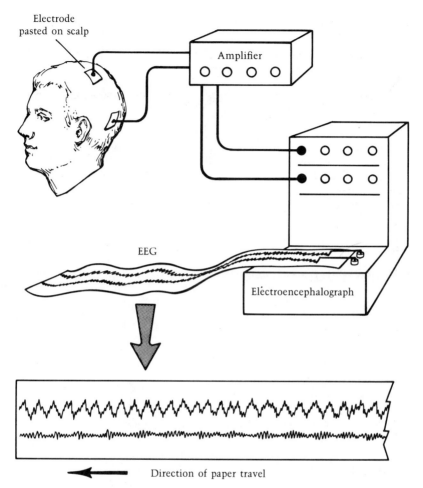

Figure 42 The general method of recording human brain activity. Activity is picked up by electrodes on the scalp, amplified and written out on a moving paper by an electroencephalograph. This records the changing voltage generated by the brain over time.

by a general lack of "waves," the activity being slight, rapid and irregular as shown in Figure 44.

There is a different characteristic EEG pattern for a person who is awake but relaxed, comfortable and with eyes closed. During relaxed wakefulness, the dominant wave frequency recorded on an EEG is between 8 and 12 oscillations per second—this is termed *alpha activity*. The EEG of a sleeping subject is characterized by large, slow

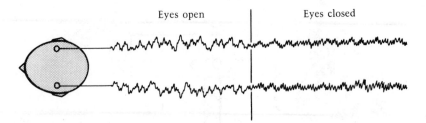

Eyes open | Eyes closed

Figure 43 EEGs showing the transition from eyes open to eyes closed in a resting human being. A characteristic "signature" is obtained with eyes closed. (Adapted from "The Electrical Activity of the Brain" by W. G. Walter. Copyright 1954 by Scientific American, Inc. All rights reserved.)

waves (Figure 44). If we observed a subject's EEG throughout a night, we would notice periods in which it looked just as it did during alert wakefulness. This phenomenon puzzled brain scientists, who named it paradoxical sleep, because the subject is sleeping but the brain

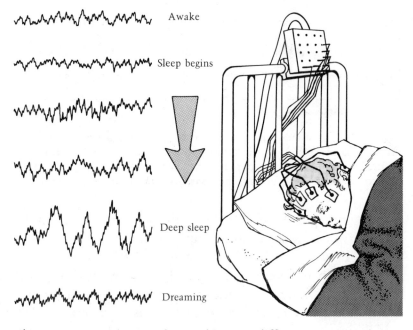

Awake

Sleep begins

Deep sleep

Dreaming

Figure 44 Typical EEGs from subjects in different states ranging from alert wakefulness to dreaming.

waves resemble those of an alert, awake person. When subjects were awakened during this period of paradoxical sleep, they usually reported that they had been in the throes of a dream. Thus, the EEG made while the subject is dreaming resembles that of an awake individual! Observation revealed that the eyes dart to and fro during dreams, giving rise to the term rapid-eye-movement (*REM*) sleep to describe the dreaming state.

Apparently we all dream, although some of us are better at recalling dreams than others. Experiments have shown that even persons who claim they never dream actually do. They apparently forget the dreams they do have. The average person has five to seven per night with each dream lasting from 10 to 40 minutes. Dreams get longer as the night progresses (Figure 45). Contrary to popular belief, we generally dream in "real time," not in super-fast or super-slow time. Many people dream in color and stereophonic sound! Most of us cannot recall the

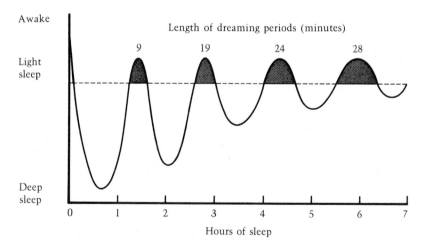

Figure 45 A typical night of sleep—a generalized graph based on all-night EEGs from many human subjects. Darkened areas indicate periods of dreaming. As can be seen, the depth of sleep progressively declines toward morning and the length of the dreaming periods increases. (Adapted from "Patterns of Dreaming" by N. Kleitman. Copyright 1960 by Scientific American, Inc. All rights reserved.)

Figure 46 Dreaming. (Adapted from "What People Dream About" by C. S. Hall. Copyright 1951 by Scientific American, Inc. All rights reserved.)

subject matter of most of our dreams. We generally remember a dream best if we are awakened in the midst of it. In detailed studies of dream content, hundreds of people were queried about the content of thousands of dreams (Figure 46). Although not all research is in agreement, the picture that emerges is that novelty has a predominant role in dreams. One-third of dream time is spent merely in going away from or toward something. A high proportion of dream time is taken up by active sports and a low proportion by dull routine. People report that the dreams following a rather dull day are sometimes spectacular and exciting, whereas the dreams following a day full of invigorating activities tend to be bland and tame. It is almost as if a dream were compensating for daily activity.

REM sleep is not limited to adults; it has been observed in newborn infants (who spend much more time in REM sleep than do adults) and many animals. A sleeping dog or cat can be observed to move its eyes rapidly, perhaps move its limbs and vocalize. The animal is exhibiting that it is in REM sleep, and although we cannot confirm it, is probably dreaming. The obvious question is, "What does a newborn baby or a dog dream about?" Unfortunately, we cannot answer this question directly. A partial answer is provided by experiments, on both human beings and animals, in which REM sleep was interrupted. That is, every time a subject went into REM sleep he or she was awakened, and thus deprived of the normal amount of dreaming. The results of the experiments were that the humans became very irritable and showed signs of mental disturbances. The symptoms disappeared following a night of uninterrupted sleep. Interestingly, the subjects, both animal and human, tended to "make up" lost REM sleep time on subsequent nights, when they exhibited evidence of half again as much REM activity as normal. An unfortunate aside is that many sleeping pills contain substances (barbiturates) that prevent or reduce REM sleep. Thus, although an individual takes a sleeping pill to obtain a good night's sleep presumably, the sleeper in fact experiences a reduction in the essential REM time and as a result may be worse off than originally. Other drugs and alcohol have a similar effect on REM sleep. An interesting theory has been proposed by Francis Crick of the Salk Institute: he suggests that REM brain activity serves to erase unnecessary memories.

We have seen that alpha activity is generally seen during relaxed wakefulness. This state is further characterized by feelings of contentment and ease. The pressures of urban life today are such that many people are looking for ways in which to cultivate feelings of peace and contentment. One such approach to this goal is for people to train themselves by using feedback techniques to produce alpha waves. The procedure is simple. An EEG electrode is pasted to the scalp. The weak signal is amplified and put into an electronic device that "recognizes" alpha activity. When alpha waves are detected, a beeping tone sounds or a light flashes. By using this information, people can train themselves to do those things that generate alpha activity. A few years ago there were many members of what has been called the "alpha cult." Admittedly many people have tried alpha training, and as with any other fad, subsequently dropped it. But for some it seems to be a satisfying means of achieving a personal goal.

Scientists are fascinated by the concept that a person can so regulate internal states as to produce changes in alpha activity or blood pressure by using biofeedback. This technique promises much in terms of relief from certain medical disorders such as high blood pressure (see pages 18–19).

The second method of recording the electrical activity of the brain is limited almost exclusively to the study of the central nervous system in laboratory animals. The electrical activity of single neurons or small numbers of neurons can be recorded by fine-tipped electrodes placed close to the particular cells. Figure 47 shows an experiment done by Karl Pribram in which the responses of single neurons in the visual cortex of monkeys are processed by computer into three dimensional maps. The major advantage of this procedure is that it allows brain scientists to specify more precisely from what area they are recording electrical activity and to study individual neurons rather than a mass of millions of cells as with the EEG.

Much of our detailed knowledge of the nervous system has come from experiments investigating the function of single neurons. The visual experiments mentioned on pages 75–77 employed single neuron recordings from the cortex of a cat's brain. Experiments more basic to the

Figure 47 The response of a single neuron in the visual cortex of a monkey. The animal is watching a moving spot while a computer records and plots the visual receptive field map in three dimensions (lower part of illustration). For this particular neuron, the unit fired most when the spot was in the center of the animal's visual field as is shown by the peak in the computer produced map. (Adapted from "The Neurophysiology of Remembering" by K. H. Pribram. Copyright 1969 by Scientific American, Inc. All rights reserved.)

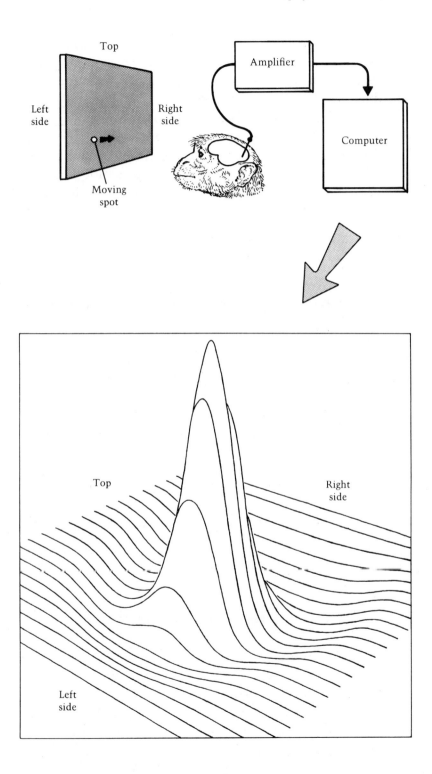

Top

Left side

Right side

Amplifier

Computer

Moving spot

Top

Right side

Left side

understanding of how a neuron produces an action potential and responds to synaptic input have used fine electrodes inserted into living neurons. Such intracellular recordings have added to our present knowledge regarding the neural mechanisms responsible for color vision, hearing and simple forms of learning, to name only a few. The brain is an assemblage of billions of neurons that act together. By understanding the activity of single neurons, we can begin to appreciate the operation of the entire brain.

☰ Summary

☰ *The electrical activity of the brain can be detected by two means. Surface recording of brain activity, which produces the EEG, has shown us that patterns of brain activity change dramatically as a person moves from one to another of the different states of wakefulness and sleep. Studies of EEGs of sleeping subjects have shown the somewhat surprising fact that when dreaming, their EEG resembles that recorded during alert wakefulness. Periods of dreaming are associated with rapid eye movements (REM) in many species. Other behavioral states produce characteristic EEG patterns. An example is the alpha wave associated with relaxed wakefulness. A technique for studying brain activity, which is generally not used in humans, is the recording of brain activity from electrodes inserted directly into the tissues of the central nervous system. Experiments using this technique have provided us with much information regarding brain mechanisms underlying sensation, perception and action.*

☰ *Electrical Stimulation of the Brain*

☰ We encountered electrical stimulation of the brain in the section where we saw that weak electric current applied to the motor cortex results in movement of some part of the body. Regions of the brain other than the motor cortex have been stimulated in both humans and animals. The most dramatic examples can be drawn from the medical treatment of persons afflicted with brain tumors. Many brain tumors must be surgically removed to prevent their causing the death of the patient. Brain surgery is delicate, for the central nervous system is very fragile and can easily be damaged. The tumors themselves increase the difficulty, as many of them are buried beneath healthy brain tissue. To minimize damage to the healthy, overlying brain, the neurosurgeon may electrically stimulate regions of the neocortex and other areas to determine their precise functions and thus be able to select areas for incision that have less crucial functions. In the course of these procedures, a great deal has been learned about brain functioning because the patients are often under only local anesthetic, and thus, can tell what they are experiencing as a result of the electrical stimulation.

As you might expect, the effect of brain stimulation depends upon what area of the brain is stimulated. Since stimulation of the motor areas was seen to produce movement, it should come as no surprise that stimulation of the visual cortex gives rise to the experience of light. Patients reported not "visions" or "scenes" but rather flashes of light. Similarly, stimulation of the somatic cortex produces sensations of touch or pressure, and activation of the auditory cortex produces the sensation of hearing. If our brain "tells us" of something in the environment, we have a tendency to believe it—even if it doesn't exist in the physical world. In other words, the only way we have of knowing the world is through our brain and sensory receptors.

At one time or another, most of us have heard or seen something when in fact nothing was there. The afterimage of a flashbulb appears to be a moving sphere of light and small children often "see" monsters in their darkened bedrooms. The heavy drinker may "see" bugs and snakes crawling over his bed—when, of course, they exist only in his or her alcohol-steeped brain. Those afflicted with mental illness may "hear" voices talking to them—yet they are not available for anyone else to hear. The point to this: to the person having the hallucinations, they are real, and often frightening.

If our sensory receptors and brain distort the world or create an alternative one, we nevertheless feel that we are receiving information about the real world. We ought not to feel that only alcoholics and the mentally ill experience such delusions: most of us hallucinate rather vividly each night in our dreams. Needless to say, a dream can be a vivid, exciting, terrifying and "real" experience—yet it is created in the brain.

If stimulating electrodes are placed over various areas of the cortex, and particularly over the association cortex, a subject may report hearing music, voices, familiar sounds, or may recall past events that had been long forgotten. By some means the electrical stimulation is drawing a buried memory out of the brain's coffer. If the stimulation is removed, the memory wanes but it returns if the stimulation is resumed. It is almost as if a phonograph needle were being repeatedly placed in the same groove of a recording. Surprisingly, if a location giving rise to a specific memory is removed during surgery, the memory is not necessarily destroyed. Obviously we cannot assume that the spot was the only repository of that memory if recall is possible following surgical removal. This suggests, on the one hand, that memories and functions are localized to a specific brain location but, on the other hand, that removal of the area does not seriously impair memory or function. This paradox is not limited to association areas and is a formidable barrier to our increased understanding of the brain.

In the 1950s a discovery was made that startled the scientific world. James Olds reported that after placing stimulating electrodes deep into the brains of rats, he could train them in a variety of tasks, the only reward being the electrical stimulation of their brain. In fact, the rats would press a lever as rapidly as they could for periods of hours, foregoing food, water and receptive mates, all to keep the electrical stimulations coming (see Figure 48). The regions

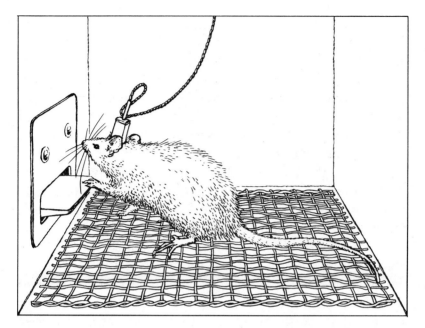

Figure 48 A rat in a Skinner box repeatedly pressing a bar, which causes electrical stimulations to be delivered to his brain.

of the brain eliciting these behaviors are certain structures in the limbic system and a part of the hypothalamus, which, as we have seen, is a major integrating system in the brain (see pages 57–58). When corresponding areas in the human brain are stimulated, the results are similar. People find it difficult to find words to describe the sensation, but report that it is pleasant and they would like it to continue.

The electrical stimulation of other areas of the brain produces diverse results. Stimulation of a region of the limbic system of a cat's brain provokes responses of "anger." The animal hisses, arches its back and seems quite fierce. The rage is only apparent, however. While the animal is exhibiting this behavior, a person can quite safely pet it. The phenomenon has been given the name "sham rage" because it is machinelike behavior. The animal is not really in a state of rage; the electrical stimulation merely produces behavior that is identical to that of rage.

Even more striking experiments have been performed with chickens having implanted brain electrodes. When brainstem structures were electrically stimulated in these birds, they performed very complex tasks. The elicited behaviors related to feeding and were very stereotyped. Each time a stimulus was given, the chicken would begin a long string of food-seeking or feeding behaviors that was totally out of context with its ongoing behavior. Apparently these animals have chains of behavior that are "programmed" into their brains. Given an appropriate stimulus these behaviors are reeled off much the same as a movie, one frame after the next.

The thought of electrodes implanted into the human brain is enough to thrill the heart of any science fiction writer. The picture of a person controlled by a mad scientist or a runaway computer is a bit extreme, even in an age of space flight and computerized dating services; however, that does not mean that the possibilities of artificial stimulation of human brains both beneficial and harmful, can be ignored. Electrodes are today being worn by a few people suffering from otherwise uncontrollable epileptic seizures. The science fiction novel *The Terminal Man,* by Michael Crichton, when stripped of its drama, is a realistic application of brain stimulation in humans. In the not-too-distant future, electrodes may be worn by the blind and deaf to restore a part of their lost capacities. Nevertheless, the control of people by means of "applied brain science" seems quite a way off into the future, if indeed it is ever possible. There are very good reasons for believing that the brain is an organ of such incredible complexity that the implantation of a number of electrodes could never begin to control its operation. In any event, the entire question of behavior control is to a large degree academic, for we are all molded by our society, parents, schooling, job and inherited and acquired status, to mention only a few. These control us in ways so effective as to quicken the pulse of any psychologist. Contrasted with these sources of control, which have been perfected over thousands of years by trial and error, any eventual attempt to control humans on the part of a neuroscientist may seem feeble by comparison.

☰ Summary

☰ *We know the world about us only through the activity of our brain. Artificial stimulation of the brain with electrical current can produce sensations normally provoked only by stimuli received from the environment. Muscles can be made to move by stimulation of the motor areas of the brain. Stimulating electrodes placed in the association areas of the brain often evoke vivid memories of past events.*

Some areas of the brain respond to electrical stimulation by producing set patterns of behavior, such as sham rage. Stimulation of certain areas of the brain produces sensations that may act as powerful positive or negative reinforcers in instrumental learning and thus can be employed to motivate animals to perform a complex series of behaviors. There are some peculiarly human implications that must be taken into account in considerations of artificial stimulation of the human brain.

☰ ***Pain***

☰ We are all familiar with pain. In general, it is something we seek to avoid at all costs. A trip to a drugstore or listening to commercials on television will soon convince everyone of the desire to avoid pain. The most widely utilized medication in the world, aspirin, is specifically designated for the relief of minor pain.

The sensation of pain results when tissue damage has occurred or is imminent. We all know that there are several types of pain: the sharp, shooting pain associated with a toothache or an injury to the surface of the body as contrasted to the dull ache of a sore muscle or joint, to the gnawing agony of intestinal cramps. In every case, how-

ever, the neural signal is rather imperative. It is very difficult to ignore a painful stimulus, and physicians specializ-
ing in the treatment of chronic pain have a great deal of
difficulty providing relief from its symptoms.

As would be expected from the behavioral data,
there are several classes of nerve fibers conveying pain
information to the central nervous system. Some are fast-
conducting and result in sharp, very localized painful sensations, whereas others are more diffuse and slow-con-
ducting and give rise primarily to the less well localized
aching variety of pain.

Phantom limb pain is a special case of painful stimuli that is experienced by many individuals unfortunate
enough to require the amputation of a limb. These individuals often report "normal" sensations, including pain,
in the limb that is no longer there. Often difficult to treat,
phantom limb pain is thought to be due to an irritation at
the stump of the cut-off nerve. The phenomenon of phantom limb pain, however, serves to illustrate one of the
principles of brain organization. That is, the only way that
the nervous system has to recognize activity occurring on
the surface of the skin, or the retina, or the cochlea, is by
where those particular fibers terminate in the brain. Stimulation of nerves that normally lead from a severed hand to
the brain will still produce sensations in the hand region of
the brain. Similarly, stimulation of fibers from the eyeball
will produce the sensation of light even though no light is
present. It is commonplace in comic-strip cartoons for an
individual to see "stars" after being bashed on the head.
This, too, is a reflection of the brain's organization such
that mechanical activation of visual regions in the brain
gives rise to the sensation that they normally transduce—
vision.

As is true of most brain processes, the experience
of pain can be modified by an individual's experience
throughout life. This is nowhere better exemplified than in
the practice of Eastern cultures. We have all been amazed
at the photographs of Eastern religious practitioners capable of walking on hot coals or lying on a bed of nails.

These are not completely hoaxes. The coals really are hot, the nails really are sharp. These individuals, when in certain psychological states, have a different set of reactions and responses to painful stimuli than do most of us. While certainly not to the same degree, most of us have experienced a similar alteration in our response to painful stimuli. Athletes have long known that a painful injury will often be disregarded in times of intense competition. Defiant children have often not noticed painful swats delivered by a parent's firm hand on their backsides when being punished for some unruly act, and remarkable degrees of agony can be endured in the name of style and fashion as is evidenced by women's high-heel shoes and men's neckties.

Several years ago an ancient Chinese treatment for alleviation of pain, either as a chronic medical condition or during surgery, came to the attention of the Western world. For many hundreds of years, the Chinese have employed acupuncture as a means of modulating and controlling pain. Acupuncture, in its usual form, has a skilled practitioner inserting slender needles into specific spots on the body and manipulating them. After a period of time, the individual may begin to experience an alleviation of pain. Initially considered a hoax, acupuncture has now been appreciated as having a scientific base. About the same time that acupuncture was drawing the attention of Western societies, a class of chemicals known as the *endorphins* and the *enkephalins* were discovered in the brain. During the acupuncture, it seems endorphins are released into the brain. Research also indicated that the powerful pain-alleviating drug, morphine, binds to endorphin receptors in the brain. Suddenly, two lines of work merged into one and clarified an important aspect of brain function—namely, that the brain contains its own pain-relieving substance, endorphin, which is normally released into the brain during times of stress. The ability to ignore pain in life threatening situations would have great survival value. The needling procedure of acupuncture released the endorphin in the absence of the stressful situation and provided relief from pain. Similarly, morphine achieved its pain-relieving properties by mimicking the action of endorphin. The other actions of morphine, particularly its ability to produce an intense state of euphoria, may also be related to the ability of morphine to bind to brain receptors. Such states of euphoria have been noted after strenuous exercise (the "runner's high") and reflect increased endorphin production triggered by the exercise.

The latter example is illustrative of the progress of scientific research. Much scientific research is not undertaken with a specific practical result in mind; rather, the search is for the basic understanding of the properties of biological systems. Often these fundamental inquiries into the nature of biology lead to important advances that can be quite beneficial to humanity. The history of science has repeatedly shown that many of the great advances that have materially benefited human society have come about by serendipitous discoveries made in basic research projects that were not necessarily seeking the outcome they found. In the case of the research discussed above, we now have an important understanding of the brain's own mechanism for regulating painful responses, information that can be utilized effectively in the alleviation of acute or chronic pain for afflicted humans.

=== Summary

Pain is a neural response intended to warn the person of imminent tissue damage, and as such is quite imperative and difficult to ignore. There are two major classes of pain: the sharp localized painful sensations from the surface of the skin and the more diffuse and aching variety of pain often associated with deeper bodily structures. These two categories of pain are carried on different neural tracts within the central nervous system.

An individual's response to pain is modified by the culture and by the immediate surroundings. Pharmacologically, relief from pain is accomplished very effectively by morphine. It has recently been discovered that opiate pain-relieving medications act on neuronal receptors within the central nervous system. These receptors are for a class of naturally occurring pain-relieving substances known as the endorphins. The morphine pain-relieving medications act upon these endorphin receptors to produce relief from pain. It has also been suggested that acupuncture, which has been shown to be effective for the relief from pain, acts by triggering the release of the body's own endorphins to promote relief from the perception of pain.

Language and the Brain

The possession of complex language is uniquely human. It is true that other animals communicate. Their communication is, however, crude in comparison with human language. Many simpler animals convey information from one to another by means of secreted chemicals that have certain odors. Other animals communicate with their vocal apparatuses as well. What animals communicate is open to speculation. It is generally agreed, however, that they communicate emotions and information directly related to survival (about danger, food and so forth). Only humans have a formal language, with rules of syntax.

Spoken language is composed of *phonemes,* the basic units of speech, that are strung together in meaningful combinations. There are about 90 different phonemes, but each language uses a unique set of only about 40 of these phonemes. The first sounds of babies incorporate many more phonemelike sounds than later in life. Their "language" behavior is shaped by those around them and they eliminate the "foreign" phonemes from their repertoire. These and other observations have led many to propose that man is innately equipped with the capacity for language. In accord with this reasoning, it may further be explained that the environment merely shapes the biological underpinning of language into a particular mode of expression, be it English, Spanish or Slavic. There are precedents to show that many complex functions are handled by genetically wired brain circuits. We discussed some relevant experiments carried out by Hubel and Wiesel on visual receptive field properties on pages 75–77. Thus, it is not inconceivable that the brain is prewired with some basic equipment for language development.

Most of the information we possess regarding brain involvement in language comes from persons suffering from brain damage. The language deficits resulting from brain damage are known as *aphasias*. The kinds of brain damage resulting in aphasia are well known. Tumors or penetrating head wounds that damage either of two neocortical locations—*Broca's* and *Wernicke's areas*—in a person's dominant hemisphere (see Figure 49) are very likely to cause aphasia, which may take one of several forms.

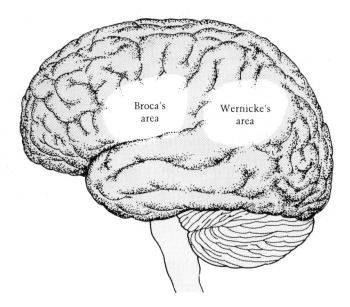

Figure 49 Speech areas of the neocortex in the dominant hemisphere of the human brain.

Table 4 Transcripts of the speech of persons suffering from aphasias. The speaker in Example A had suffered damage to the anterior language cortex (Broca's area), the speaker in B damage to the posterior language cortex (Wernicke's area).

Example A	"I am taking.....ah......Sherriks......ah....... Sherring's mixture (laugh). It's easier from me to...... stalk......talk staccato and breaking up each word ......into sentences.......breaking up sentences into words provided they have ah......not many syllables. Ah, syllable is hard.......Precise words that I have trouble with are Republican and Epics.........Epis ....capalian."
Example B	"Well, I thought thing I am going to tell is about my operation and it is not about all I can tell is about the preparation the had was already the time was when they had me to get ready that is they shaved off all my hair was and a few odd parts of pencil they give me in the fanny."

Sources:
Example A from E. G. Lenneberg, *Biological Foundations of Language*. New York: Wiley (1967), pg. 195.
Example B from W. Penfield, *Speech and Brain Mechanisms*. Princeton, N.J.: Princeton University Press (1959), pg. 146.

The results of hundreds of case studies have suggested that Broca's area is responsible for the "output processing" of language, or more precisely, that it contains the rules by which a speaker codes ideas into spoken language. Damage to Broca's area results in broken speech that is produced with great difficulty. Meaning, however, is preserved in Broca's aphasia (Table 4). Wernicke's area, on the other hand, seems to be involved in the comprehension of language. In Wernicke's aphasia, the patient often produces a torrent of words that, however, conveys no meaning. These effects are seen only if the damage is in the dominant hemisphere. In a right-handed person, the dominant hemisphere is the left. Aphasia in an adult is almost certainly permanent, but a child suffering from aphasia may completely recover if the other side of his brain is undamaged. Apparently the brain of a child is sufficiently adaptable to compensate for damage to a part of it.

Electrical recording from the scalp overlying the cortical language areas has shown that brain potentials evoked by words are more pronounced over the dominant hemisphere. This is in accord with the clinical findings of the effects of brain damage to the dominant hemisphere.

Interesting experiments have been performed showing differences in brain activity that are associated with word meaning. In such experiments the subjects hear a single word that can be interpreted two ways, that is, an ambiguous word. The brain activity from language centers of the cortex shows marked differences depending upon which of the two meanings is perceived (Figure 50).

===== Summary

There are two neocortical areas of the brain that appear to be specialized for language. One is for the input processing of language and the other for the output processing. Much of our knowledge of the functions of these areas has come from persons whose brains have been damaged in one or both of these areas. Electrical recording of brain activity has contributed to our knowledge of brain processes in language.

===== ***Brain Aging***

What happens to the brain as we grow old? One clue to changes that occur within the brain can be seen from an examination of changes in behavior with age. We are all familiar with the stereotype of the aged individual: somewhat befuddled, forgetful, living in the past, disoriented. While undoubtedly unfair to a great many of the elderly, such a characterization does depict an all too common consequence of aging.

These behavioral changes with aging—loss of memory, disorientation and the like—would suggest a widespread involvement in the brain rather than a single location. An exaggeration of this process can be seen in individuals afflicted with *Alzheimer's disease,* a common

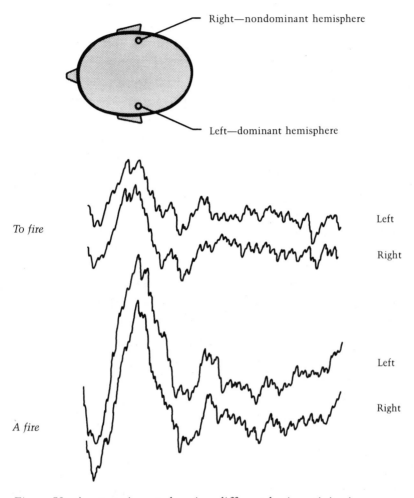

Figure 50 An experiment showing different brain activity in response to the word *fire* depending on whether it is interpreted as a verb (*to fire*) or a noun (*a fire*). The lines shown were obtained by taking the algebraic average of many individual EEGs from the language cortex on the left hemisphere and from an analogous location on the right hemisphere.

and devastating disorder resulting in senility. In the brain of the Alzheimer patient, widespread destruction of neurons in the cerebral cortex can be seen. Coupled with the widespread destruction and death of neurons is the presence of a unique formation in the brain of these patients which has come to be diagnostic of the disease. The underlying cause of Alzheimer's disease is not understood.

Many believe it to be an acceleration of the normal aging process although it actually represents a distinct disease process in itself. These pronounced changes in behavior and in brain structure are seen to a minor degree in the elderly not afflicted with Alzheimer's disease.

Not all individuals suffer equally from the ravages of aging. What is it that differentiates one individual from the other? Why should one individual show the mental strains of aging while a neighbor equally as aged is as alert as a twenty-year-old? The answers to these questions are not known. What is known is that the cells of the brain never replace themselves when lost. By the age of seventy or eighty, a significant number of all of the neurons originally present in an individual's brain may have been lost. The reason for the death of neurons, which does not occur only in old age but also affects younger individuals, is not known. Certain kinds of abuse, for example alcoholic intoxication, will lead to an accelerated death among neurons no matter what the age of the drinker. Some diseases, in addition to Alzheimer's disease, also result in cell death.

At first encounter, it would appear that neuronal death is something to be avoided at all costs. However, massive neuronal death is a rather normal part of the development of the nervous system in early life. In the developing human brain, many more neurons are initially produced than can be accommodated into the nervous system. Therefore, in early life, neurons die at an astounding rate at the same time that others are elaborating and forming their dendritic branching patterns and axonal fiber pathways. The process of neuronal death can be seen as a process that is normally occurring at some level throughout life. One theory suggests that neurons that are unsuccessful in establishing synaptic contact with targets are programmed to die. Remember, too, that even in the aging individual, those remaining neurons are continually growing and expanding their connectivity with other elements in the circuit. It is possible that the reason for this continued expansion of their synaptic connectivity is to compensate for the death of some of their "neighbors."

===== Summary

===== *The behavioral changes associated with aging often take the form of loss of memory, disorientation and a decrease in mental abilities. In extreme form and coupled with other difficulties are the symptoms of an illness called Alzheimer's disease, a common disease of the aged associated with senility. The causative agents in Alzheimer's disease are unknown whereas the changes in the brain with this disease have been well studied. In the normal brain, aging is accompanied by a loss in the number of neurons in the central nervous system but a continued elaboration of the surviving neurons. It may be that this death of neurons is a normal consequence of neuronal death seen to occur soon after birth.*

Consciousness and Awareness

===== Psychology has been defined as the study of consciousness. By this is meant the mental life of an individual—feelings, sensations, thoughts and whatever else it is that goes on within our skulls every day. The brain scientist cannot explain the workings of the "mind" ... yet. The sum total of our consciousness—of our "mind"—is the product of very complicated brain processes. We are only now beginning to learn how the brain works in performing simple tasks such as responding to sensory information and generating movement. The brain scientist is still at a loss when it comes to explaining in terms of brain mechanisms our desires, ambitions or other feelings. This does not mean that these feelings are not the result of brain activity—they most certainly are. The brain mechanisms associated with them are simply poorly understood at this time.

Considerable progress in our understanding has been achieved by studying humans afflicted with various brain disorders. Roger Sperry has provided a dramatic demonstration of the differences in function between the dominant and nondominant hemispheres. His subjects

Figure 51 Split-brain operations. A top view of the brain shows the interconnecting axons that are severed in split-brain operations. In the lower part of the illustration, a split-brain man tests the verbal ability of his nondominant (right) hemisphere. In the test a picture of a spoon is flashed to the right hemisphere; with his left hand the subject examines various hidden objects by touch, seeking the spoon. The right hemisphere can perform the task correctly but cannot readily verbalize what the object is.

were several neurosurgical patients whose two hemispheres had been surgically disconnected as a treatment for epilepsy (Figure 51). The two hemispheres are connected by bundles of axons whose function is to relay information back and forth between the two hemispheres. Without this crossflow of information, it is impossible for the two hemispheres to work together. It is as if two pianists were attempting to play a piano duet without being able to hear one another. Following surgery a patient has within the skull in effect, two brains operating independently. The disconnection of the two hemispheres, which is termed a *split-brain operation*, is drastic surgery and is only done in rare cases of epilepsy resistant to other forms of treatment.

Surprisingly, the split-brain patients behave almost normally in everyday situations because both hemispheres receive simultaneous, noncontradictory information. Only in laboratory tests do the special functions of each hemisphere show themselves. The dominant hemisphere can be shown to be specialized for language, computation and logical thinking. When split-brain patients speak they are using the dominant hemisphere. The nondominant hemisphere is silent. This mute hemisphere deals with music, the location of objects in space and other nonverbal tasks. Tests have shown that split-brain patients can direct behavior and "think" in either hemisphere. Thus, consciousness is not a feature of one hemisphere over the other. Although both hemispheres can "think," they do not necessarily carry out the same functions or express the

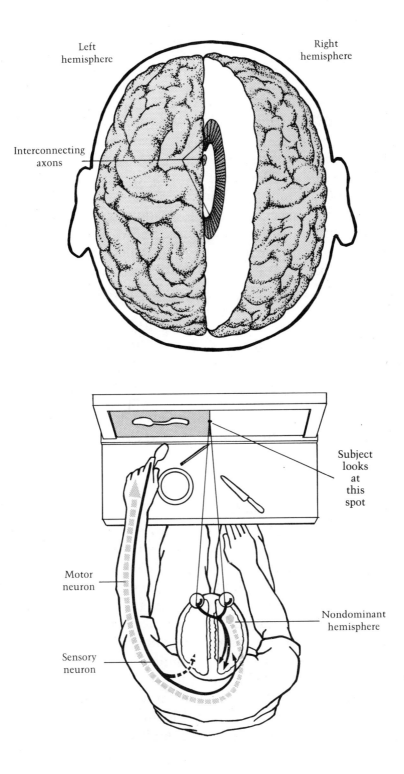

Left
hemisphere

Right
hemisphere

Interconnecting
axons

Subject
looks
at
this
spot

Motor
neuron

Nondominant
hemisphere

Sensory
neuron

results of their "thought" in the same manner. For example, an embarrassing stimulus (a nude man) was presented, along with many neutral stimuli, only to the nondominant hemisphere. The patient, a woman, reacted to the embarrassing stimulus by blushing, squirming in her chair and laughing nervously. When asked what it was she had seen, she could not identify the embarrassing stimulus. In this case the verbal, dominant hemisphere had not seen the stimulus, and since the interconnecting axons were severed, had no access to the information. The verbal hemisphere, in fact, acted as a "passive" observer of the behavior produced by the nonverbal hemisphere. For its part the nondominant hemisphere, although not able to "verbalize" what it had seen, was able to produce emotional reactions to the embarrassing stimulus.

In another situation the two hemispheres were simultaneously given the same task to perform—assembling a geometrical puzzle. The dominant hemisphere primarily controlled the right hand, and the nondominant hemisphere the left. As you might expect, the nondominant hemisphere was superior in this task entailing perception of spatial relations among objects. When instructed to assemble the puzzle, the dominant hemisphere tried to do so. The total result was that the nondominant hemisphere's hand would make good progress on the task only to have the dominant hemisphere's hand mess it up. The two hemispheres were in conflict to the extent that the left hand would actually try to restrain the right hand. Such conflict is not seen in the normal brain in which the two hemispheres communicate with each other to produce integrated behavior. As we have seen, the split-brain person is deprived of this ability. As a result the two hemispheres can be taught or can develop incompatible responses to a single stimulus, resulting in conflict between the behavioral responses called for by the two "brains." The split-brain patients, although few in number, have shown us that the functions of the two hemispheres are separate. Each hemisphere is capable of complex mental operations.

Such patients may be said to quite literally possess two brains or even two separate "consciousnesses."

Our awareness of the world about us is in a continuous state of flux. We drift from being alert and attentive to being bored and disinterested, with alarming speed. In fact, some states of awareness—such as sleeping—are characterized by very little "awareness" of the external world. Yet while sleeping we experience very vivid impressions of an external world not really there. Such periods of dreaming will take place in an altered state of awareness. Few would deny the apparent reality of a vivid dream. Yet all of us (except small children) recognize that the dream was unreal—that it occurred in an altered state of awareness.

Drugs are powerful awareness-altering agents. Their power to alter brain function comes from the fact that many of them mimic or oppose such chemical reactions as synaptic transmission in the brain. Other drugs enhance or depress activity in certain areas of the brain in order to produce their effect. Although there exist many ways to alter awareness (education, music, sports, travel, conversation), drugs remain as powerful awareness-altering agents. This is due in part to the intensity of their effect and in part to their fast action.

Drugs and Behavior

We are a nation of pill takers. Taking drugs has both beneficial and detrimental effects, but most of us would agree that the beneficial far outweigh the detrimental. Nevertheless, some drugs are consumed for decidedly nonmedical reasons. The history of man is well documented regarding drugs that were used in former times, often as part of religious pursuits, to induce altered states of awareness. But never before has such a variety of drugs existed with the power to change behavior or the experience of living. Table 5 gives the major categories of "psychoactive" drugs and their effects.

Table 5 Psychoactive drugs

Type	Examples	Effect
Narcotic	Morphine Heroin	Relieve pain, promote feelings of well-being; addictive
Stimulant	Caffeine Nicotine Amphetamines	Relieve fatigue, increase awareness, decrease appetite; produce anxiety; moderately addictive
Psychogenic	LSD Mescaline Psilosibin Marijuana	Produce psychosis-like states; hallucinations; distortions of space and time; nonaddictive
Psychotherapeutic	Antipsychotics reserpine chlorpromazine	Reduce psychotic behavior
	Antianxiety drugs meprobamate chlordiazepoxide	Act as tranquilizers
	Antidepressants imipramine	Reduce depression; other effects similar to those of the stimulants

Narcotic drugs These drugs have been known for centuries as powerful agents for relieving pain and producing a marked sense of well-being. These drugs, the opiates—morphine and heroin—are the most addictive agents known. Addiction is not completely understood but involves a powerful biological need for the substance. As discussed on page 151, we now know something of the neural basis of opiate addiction. If drugs are withheld from an addict, he or she suffers withdrawal symptoms, which range in severity but are all acutely unpleasant; withdrawal effects can even be fatal. The most potently addicting drugs are usually those whose withdrawal effects are most severe.

In contrast to these biologically addicting drugs are the psychologically "addicting" drugs such as marijuana. These are not addicting in the physiological sense of the word. Regular marijuana users experience no physiological symptoms if the pattern of use is broken. They continue to use the drug because they like it.

Stimulant drugs Some of the most common drugs used in the United States are the stimulants. The milder forms include caffeine, which is in coffee, tea and soda, and nicotine, which is in tobacco. These stimulants act to excite the brain, alleviate fatigue and serve as a general "pick-me-up." They are relatively safe and have few side effects for most people. (It is not the nicotine in cigarettes that causes cancer; other agents present in burning tobacco are carcinogenic.)

The most abused of the stimulants are the amphetamines. These are powerful agents used to alleviate fatigue, increase awareness, decrease appetite and reduce the need for sleep. They produce euphoria (a feeling of elation, a "high"), often followed by depression. These drugs have been abused. Continued overuse of amphetamines results in a condition similar to psychosis (a defective or lost contact with reality); furthermore, these drugs are addicting. Their medical uses are in combatting abnormal drowsiness and serving as an aid to weight loss.

Psychogenic drugs These drugs are capable of creating psychosis-like states. Members of this group include LSD, mescaline, psilosibin and marijuana. Many of these drugs have been around for centuries. In fact at one time marijuana was prescribed by American physicians for their patients. The drugs can produce hallucinations (visions of objects that are not present), euphoria and psychosis-like behavior.

LSD and its derivatives are the most powerful and dangerous drugs in this group. They have powerful and peculiar distorting effects on sensory experience. The resulting behavior can also be bizarre. Many persons have been hospitalized as the result of an unpleasant LSD experience. Many others have reported that symptoms felt while under the effect of LSD spontaneously recur later.

Marijuana is a mild psychogenic drug with few side effects. Its main effect is to produce a mild state of euphoria. It exists in a concentrated form as hashish, which is nearly as powerful as LSD. Marijuana, like the other psychogenic drugs, is not biologically addictive.

Alcohol The drug that has the most widespread use and the greatest cultural acceptance in the United States is alcohol. In small amounts, alcohol appears to stimulate the appetite and produce a mild euphoria, and has few side effects, although in larger amounts it acts as a depressant drug. In greater amounts or when taken by chronic alcoholics, the situation is altogether different. There are distortions of time and space, lack of coordination, impaired perception, and liver and brain damage. Alcohol is considered to be responsible for a large share of the tens of thousands of annual highway fatalities in the United States. It must be considered a dangerous and potentially addicting drug when consumed in large amounts.

Psychotherapeutic drugs The era of the insane asylum is gone, partly because of an awakening of humanity but partly because of a revolution in drug technology. No drug known today can cure mental illness. The action of psychotherapeutic drugs is like that of aspirin—offering symptomatic relief. That they do not cure mental illness does not mean that medicine has achieved a false victory. Indeed aspirin makes tolerable a splitting headache and allows the person to function in a near-normal manner. So it is with these drugs.

The psychotherapeutics are of three varieties. The antipsychotics reduce the severity and duration of psychotic behavior. This mechanism of action appears to involve modulating the effect of certain of the brain's neurotransmitters. The antianxiety drugs, or tranquilizers, produce an effect similar to mild doses of alcohol but without the sleep-producing effects. These drugs are prescribed when it is desirable to reduce anxiety and produce some euphoria. The last variety of psychotherapeutic drug is the antidepressant. These drugs are used in cases of severe depression (undue sadness with no cause). Their effect is similar to that of the amphetamines but longer lasting.

In using any drug, whether it be for recreation or on doctor's orders, the prudent person should recall that these are chemicals foreign to the body and caution should be exercised in their use. Drugs are the result of wonderful scientific advances but should not be misused or abused.

≡ Summary

The sum total of all of our brain processes operating together determines consciousness. Brain scientists are only now beginning to understand the brain mechanisms that underlie consciousness. Split-brain operations have shown quite dramatically that there is a considerable division of labor between the hemispheres of the normal human brain. The dominant hemisphere is specialized for language, computation and logical thinking. The nondominant hemisphere is mute and responsible for the location of objects in space. Normally, however, the two hemispheres communicate with each other to produce an integrated output. Following surgical disconnection of the two hemispheres, however, it is possible to see the specialization of each.

Our awareness of the world around us is in continuous flux. We fluctuate from wakefulness to sleep, from arousal to lethargy. Some of the more potent external modulators of awareness are the drugs that act upon the brain. There are narcotic drugs, stimulants, psychogenic drugs, alcohol and psychotherapeutic drugs. Like most advances in science, drugs are both very beneficial and potentially harmful if abused.

The brain may be the most complex thing in the universe. Its operation is certainly more complicated than the most intricate computer. The behaviors that it produces are infinite in their variety. The brain sciences have only begun to explain the functioning of the brain. We may never get to the point where we "understand" its operation completely. Men and women have been trying to understand our species and its situation for centuries. Judging by our present condition, beset with war and violence, poverty and prejudice, pollution and exploitation, these efforts have not succeeded. If the brain sciences can provide any understanding at all of the human race, then the effort is decidedly worthwhile.

It is hoped that the reader of this book has gained some appreciation of his or her own nervous system and of the fact that all that we are and do is the result of brain activity. If so, then the book has succeeded in its mission.

Suggestions for Further Reading

Barron, F.; Jarvik, M. E.; and Bunnell, S., Jr. "The Hallucinogenic Drugs." *Scientific American,* April 1964. (Offprint 484)

Brazier, M. A. B. "The Analysis of Brain Waves." *Scientific American,* June 1962

Gazzaniga, M. S. "The Split Brain in Man." *Scientific American,* August 1966. (Offprint 508)

Grinspoon, L. "Marihuana." *Scientific American,* December 1969. (Offprint 524)

Hall, C. S. "What People Dream About." *Scientific American,* May 1951.

Harlow, H. F. "Love in Infant Monkeys." *Scientific American,* June 1959. (Offprint 429)

Harlow, H. J., and Harlow, M. K. "Social Deprivation in Monkeys." *Scientific American,* November 1962. (Offprint 473)

Jouvet, M. "The States of Sleep." *Scientific American,* February 1967. (Offprint 504)

Kimura, D. "The Asymmetry of the Human Brain." *Scientific American,* March 1973. (Offprint 554)

Kleitman, N. "Patterns of Dreaming." *Scientific American,* November 1960. (Offprint 460)

Kohler, I. "Experiments with Goggles." *Scientific American,* May 1962. (Offprint 465)

Olds, J. "Pleasure Centers in the Brain." *Scientific American,* October 1956. (Offprint 30)

Sperry, R. W. "The Great Cerebral Commissure." *Scientific American,* January 1964. (Offprint 174)

Sperry, R. W. "Hemisphere Deconnection and Unity in Conscious Awareness." *American Psychologist* 23 (1968), pp. 723–733

Springer, S. P., and Deutsch, G. *Left Brain, Right Brain.* San Francisco: W. H. Freeman, 1981

Teyler, T. J. *Altered States of Awareness.* San Francisco: W. H. Freeman, 1972

von Holst, E., and von Saint Paul, U. "Electrically Controlled Behavior." *Scientific American,* March 1962. (Offprint 464)

≡ *Glossary*

action potential: the nerve impulse, a transient alteration of the neural membrane that allows a brief
  flow of ions. The action potential travels down an
  axon and can be measured electrically.

adaptation: the tendency of a sensory neuron to cease
  responding to a nonchanging stimulus.

alpha activity: brain activity of a particular frequency
  associated with relaxed wakefulness.

Alzheimer's disease: a common and devastating disorder resulting in senility. The neocortex is particularly involved in this form of dementia.

androgen: a male gonadal hormone.

aphasia: a disturbance of language. There are many
  forms of it, such as difficulties in speaking, reading
  or understanding.

association neocortex: a portion of the cortex concerned with complex processes such as the manipulation of symbolic elements.

auditory canal: the external ear canal leading to the eardrum.

autonomic nervous system: the portion of the nervous system that regulates physiological functions
  not normally under conscious control, such as heart
  rate and blood pressure.

axon: a process of a neuron, often quite long, that can release chemical transmitters from its end to affect an adjoining neuron or muscle.

basilar membrane: a membrane in the cochlea upon which are found the hair cells of the inner ear.

behavioral plasticity: modifiability of behavior as the result of experience (e.g., through classical conditioning or habituation). It does not refer to unlearned changes provoked by such factors as fatigue.

biofeedback: information communicated to an organism by artificial means about one of its physiological responses (e.g., heart rate) in order that the subject may attempt to modify the response.

brainstem: a collection of neural structures located at the base of the brain closely associated with the autonomic nervous system.

Broca's area: a component of the language cortex involved with the generation of language. Damage to Broca's area results in slow, labored speech but with meaning intact.

cell body: enlarged region of a neuron that contains the nucleus.

central nervous system: the brain and spinal cord.

cerebellum: a neural center for the coordination of movement.

chemical senses: the sensory systems concerned with smell and taste. They respond to molecules suspended in air or liquid.

circadian rhythms: cyclic variations in physiological states. Often entrained to the light/dark patterns, examples include body temperature, sleep patterns and hormone levels.

classical conditioning: the establishment of a new response to a neutral stimulus after repeated associations with a meaningful stimulus.

cloning: production of new organisms without sexual reproduction. Under certain conditions, DNA transplanted from a cell of one organism into an egg cell of another organism will direct the "construction" of an organism or tissue identical to the donor.

cochlea: the structure of the inner ear containing the sound-transducing hair cells.

cognitive behavior: complicated behaviors and mental processes—characteristic of humans—including thinking, deciding, reasoning, planning and reflecting.

conditioned response: the learned response to a neutral stimulus in classical conditioning.

cones: photoreceptor neurons of the retina that operate in daylight and convey color information.

contact comfort: the force that binds an infant monkey to a mother monkey.

control: elimination of the effects of extraneous variables on a phenomenon.

control group: a group of subjects maintained throughout an experiment without special treatment to provide a basis against which the behavior of other groups can be evaluated.

cornea: the transparent tissue through which light is crudely focused onto the retina of the eye. The lens performs the final, precise focusing.

cortex: a layer of neurons on the surface of the brain.

dendrite: a many-branched process of a neuron that conveys information to the cell body. A dendrite may be associated with many synapses.

diabetes: a disease characterized by insufficient amounts of insulin in the blood leading to tissue starvation.

electroencephalogram (EEG): a graphic record of the brain's electrical activity measured through the scalp.

endocrine gland: a gland that releases a hormone into the blood.

endorphin (enkephalin): a class of chemicals naturally present in the brain that have pain-relieving properties. The drug morphine binds to the receptors for these chemicals.

estrogen: a female gonadal hormone.

estrous cycle: cyclic changes in gonadal hormone levels and behavior.

ethologist: a scientist who is primarily concerned with the study of animal behavior.

extrapyramidal system: one of two systems for transmittal of motor output from the brain.

field method: the observation of phenomena in their natural setting.

forebrain: the largest subdivision of the human brain. It comprises the cortex, thalamus, hypothalamus, pituitary and limbic system. Phylogenetically, it is the most recent brain structure.

fovea: a small area of the retina containing tightly packed cones. The fovea is used in looking directly at an object.

frontal lobe: a division of the cortex, site of cortical motor areas.

gonadotrophic hormone: a hormone released by the pituitary gland causing an increase in activity of the gonads.

habituation: the reduction of response to an unchanging stimulus that is repeatedly presented.

homeostasis: maintenance of conditions in the body within a narrow range by a collection of mechanisms including hunger, thirst, activity, temperature-regulating mechanisms and so forth.

homunculus: the receptortopic representation of the body in the motor and somatic sensory areas of the cortex. Each representation is that of a disproportioned figure.

hormone: the chemical product of an endocrine gland.

hypothalamus: a tiny portion of the brain concerned with the regulation of eating, drinking, temperature and other functions.

innate behavior sequence: a complex sequence of behaviors that appears to the human observer to be purposeful. It is elicited by a specific stimulus and is primarily under genetic influence.

instrumental learning: a method of altering behavior in which the response to be established is reinforced when it appears.

interneurons: neurons specialized to integrate information from other neurons and to activate appropriate response patterns. The bulk of the human brain is composed of interneurons.

kinesthetic sense: the sensory system concerned with the orientation and location of the different parts of the body.

laboratory method: the examination of a phenomenon in an environment in which the variables are controlled.

limbic system: a collection of many neural structures involved with emotionality, motivation and perhaps aggression and memory.

manipulation of symbolic elements: complex human behaviors entailing the use of abstract symbols (such as language).

meninges: the membranes covering the brain.

motor neurons: neurons specialized to direct the action of the body's musculature.

myofibrils: the contractile portion of the muscle. Each muscle has millions of myofibrils. During contraction the proteins in the myofibrils slide past one another, shortening the muscle.

neocortex: the wrinkled sheet of neurons covering much of the rest of the brain. Higher perceptual processes and cognition occur in the neocortex.

neuron: a nerve cell (or brain cell). Neurons are cells specialized for communication and integration.

nerve: a bundle of neural processes found outside the brain, usually axons.

occipital lobe: a division of the cortex, site of cortical visual areas.

olfactory bulb: an extension of the brain concerned with the sense of smell.

ossicles: three tiny bones linking the eardrum with the cochlea.

parasympathetic division: the portion of the autonomic nervous system that operates to conserve and maintain bodily resources.

parietal lobe: a division of the cortex, site of cortical body sense areas.

peripheral nervous system: the network of nerves and receptors lying outside of the brain and spinal cord. It comprises the autonomic nervous system and the somatic nervous system.

phoneme: the basic units of speech. There are about 90 different phonemes although each language uses only about 40 of these phonemes.

photochemicals: chemicals in the rods and cones whose molecular configurations are altered upon exposure to light.

pinna: the portion of the ear visible to the eye. Its function is to direct sound waves into the ear.

pituitary: the master gland. It works closely with the hypothalamus to regulate such functions as reproductive cycles, tissue growth, temperature and water balance.

progesterone: a female gonadal hormone.

pyramidal system: one of two systems for transmittal of motor output from the brain.

receptor: in sensory systems, the specialized neurons that transduce sensory signals into neural impulses; in synaptic transmission, the protein molecule that binds the neurotransmitter.

receptortopic: representation of a receptor surface. For example, the body surface is represented on the parietal lobe of the cortex.

reductionist: a person who seeks to explain a phenomenon by reducing it to the parts of which it is constituted.

reflex: an unlearned reaction of an organism to a stimulus, often in response to a potentially harmful stimulus.

reinforcer: a stimulus used in instrumental learning that tends to increase the probability of repetition of the response preceding it (e.g., food, praise). A reinforcer can also be negative (e.g., electric shock, criticism), in which case the probability of repetition of the preceding response is decreased.

releaser: a stimulus capable of eliciting an innate behavior sequence.

REM sleep: rapid-eye-movement sleep, associated with periods of EEG activation and dreaming.

repeatability: the capability of an experiment to be repeated, in order that the original findings may be verified or invalidated.

replication: *see **repeatability**.*

reticular formation: a diffuse area of the core of the brainstem concerned with arousal and alerting.

retina: the light-sensitive portion of the eye.

rods: photoreceptor neurons of the retina that operate under dim illumination and convey only black and white information.

sensitization: an augmentation of a response to a stimulus.

sensory neurons: neurons specialized to transduce sensory stimuli (light, sound, pressure) into neural potentials.

somatic nervous system: a subdivision of the peripheral nervous system concerned with relaying movement commands to muscle, and relaying sensory information from receptor to brain.

somatic sensory system: the sensory system concerned with sensations at the body surface such as touch and temperature.

spinal cord: an extension of the central nervous system that contains motor neurons which supply the trunk and limb muscles, and nerve fibers conveying sensory information to the brain. It is encased in the vertebrae.

split-brain operations: the surgical disconnection of the two hemispheres.

sympathetic division: the portion of the autonomic nervous system that operates to mobilize bodily resources for action.

synapse: the synaptic gap and the adjoining axonal and dendritic membranes.

synaptic gap: the gap between the axon of one neuron and the dendrite or cell body of another. Neurotransmitter is released into the synaptic gap where it affects the second neuron.

taste buds: specialized structures for taste located primarily on the tongue.

taxis: an unlearned movement toward or away from a stimulus.

tectorial membrane: a stiff membrane opposite the basilar membrane of the cochlea. Sensory hair cells are stimulated by vibrations that cause them to rub against this membrane.

temporal lobe: a division of the cortex, site of cortical auditory arcas.

thalamus: a sensory relay area in the brain that is also concerned with arousal and attention.

transmitter: the chemical released from an axon that influences an adjoining neuron or muscle. Transmitters can be excitatory or inhibitory.

variables: environmental or genetic factors that are capable of influencing the outcome of an experiment. It is desirable to control for the effects of variables.

vasectomy: the surgical removal of a part of the vas deferens (the structure that carries sperm).

vertebrae: the bony skeleton encasing the spinal cord.

vestibular sense: organs near the ear that allow one to maintain balance.

visual cliff: a device for testing an organism's fear of depth.

Wernicke's area: a component of the language cortex involved with the understanding of language. Damage here results in difficulties in producing meaningful speech.

Index